PETERSON GUIDE TO

BIRD
IDENTIFICATION—
IN 12 STEPS

PETERSON GUIDE TO
BIRD IDENTIFICATION—
IN 12 STEPS

Steve N. G. Howell

AND

Brian L. Sullivan

HOUGHTON MIFFLIN HARCOURT
BOSTON • NEW YORK • 2018

For information about permission to reproduce selections from this book,
write to Permissions, Houghton Mifflin Harcourt Publishing Company, 3 Park
Avenue, 19th Floor, New York, New York 10016.

hmhco.com

Library of Congress Cataloging-in-Publication Data is available.

ISBN 978-1-328-66206-4

Book design by Eugenie S. Delaney

Printed in China

SCP 10 9 8 7 6 5 4 3 2 1

ROGER TORY PETERSON INSTITUTE
OF NATURAL HISTORY

Continuing the work of Roger Tory Peterson through Art, Education, and Conservation

In 1984, the Roger Tory Peterson Institute of Natural History (RTPI) was founded in Peterson's hometown of Jamestown, New York, as an educational institution charged by Peterson with preserving his lifetime body of work and making it available to the world for educational purposes.

RTPI is the only official institutional steward of Roger Tory Peterson's body of work and his enduring legacy. It is our mission to foster understanding, appreciation, and protection of the natural world. By providing people with opportunities to engage in nature-focused art, education, and conservation projects, we promote the study of natural history and its connections to human health and economic prosperity.

Art—Using Art to Inspire Appreciation of Nature
The RTPI Archives contains the largest collection of Peterson's art in the world—iconic images that continue to inspire an awareness of and appreciation for nature.

Education—Explaining the Importance of Studying Natural History
We need to study, firsthand, the workings of the natural world and its importance to human life. Local surroundings can provide an engaging context for the study of natural history and its relationship to other disciplines such as math, science, and language. Environmental literacy is everybody's responsibility—not just experts and special interests.

Conservation—Sustaining and Restoring the Natural World
RTPI works to inspire people to choose action over inaction, and engages in meaningful conservation research and actions that transcend political and other boundaries. Our goal is to increase awareness and understanding of the natural connections between species, habitats, and people—connections that are critical to effective conservation.

For more information, and to support RTPI, please visit rtpi.org.

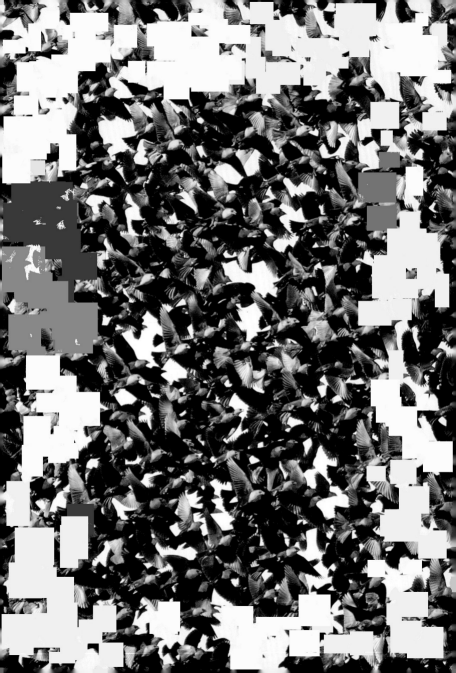

CONTENTS

What Is This Book?

These days, millions of people around the world watch birds. It's a great excuse to get outside in the fresh air, to explore the remarkable world around you. And a big part of the fun is putting a name to the bird you are watching: What kind of bird is that? *But how do you go about this seemingly simple quest?*

Not everyone has a mentor to guide them in understanding how to observe birds and approach the identification process. And not everyone has the time or dedication or even wants to become a full-time professional birder, which requires a huge amount of work. Most people spend their days working at something other than birding, so when they have free time they don't want to work; they want to relax, to enjoy themselves. As professional birders, we subscribe to Kenn Kaufman's definition that "a good birder is somebody who enjoys birding." That said, most people who enjoy birding also like to learn as they go along.

To this end, there are many useful books and online projects out there to help you—even classes you can take to become more proficient at identifying birds. But still, when you look at a field guide there's so much choice—hundreds of species, some with different plumages for males, females, immatures, even seasonal plumages. It can be overwhelming.

The good news is that you already know a lot about birds, whether you realize it or not. One of us is from Wales, and among other things the Welsh have been defined as simple machines for turning beer into

OPPOSITE: Palm Warbler. *Monterey County, California, 13 November 2016.*

urine. This may help explain why we often like to start from the simplest level and move upward—it's the only way to go.

The twelve steps thus start with the basics, things that many people don't think about or simply take for granted; then we build logically into a manageable framework that can help anyone in his or her goal to identify and appreciate birds. We offer this book as a resource to people at all levels of interest, because one of the great things about birding is the infinite capacity for learning. If you're fairly new to the world of birds, this book will help you understand the fundamentals of observation and the identification (or ID) process. If you're a more experienced birder, this book will help you step back from your years in the field and refresh your thoughts on how you watch and identify birds.

We include some things that may be challenging for beginning birders, and others that may seem too basic for those more advanced, but this is intentional. We have attempted to organize the fundamentals in a way that can help a broad range of people who are enthusiastic about birds. So bear with us if a concept such as "oscine" is completely new and daunting, or if we have belabored something obvious from your first days of birding.

Last, but importantly, this book isn't intended as a one-stop shop for how to identify birds—it should be read and used in conjunction with your field guides. But field guides cover only so much (or so little) of the story, and here we expand upon the information they provide. So without further ado, let's step right into the process of bird identification—it's easier than you might think!

OPPOSITE: Whether you're among a group of teenagers in the Colorado Rockies (top) or a group of adults taking a two-week cruise around Cape Horn at the southern tip of South America (bottom), birding is a great way to get outside and see the world. Few hobbies offer so much for all ages of people from different cultures and walks of life. The twelve-step program we cover in this book outlines a pathway to enable anyone to get into, or get more out of, the world of watching, identifying, and enjoying birds.

STEP 1

You Can't Get There from Here (Taxonomy)

Look, up in the sky: It's a bird. It's a plane. It's Superman!

Have you ever been fooled, at least briefly, by something that wasn't a bird but at first you thought it was? A leaf, a snag, a piece of trash, a flyingfish even? Perhaps we could ask who *hasn't* been. Sadly, there is no magic recipe to avoid this—it just happens less with practice. Basically, there are two kinds of birders: those who make mistakes and those who pretend they don't.

Years ago, during a month of birding in Israel, Steve visited a desert kibbutz in search of the little-known Hume's Tawny Owl (today known as Desert Owl, *Strix hadorami*). As dusk fell, a fairly large owl came flying along above the fence around the kibbutz, dimly lit by lights from the buildings. The owl was dark overall, and clearly not a Barn Owl—wow,

OPPOSITE: You don't need to be a professional taxonomist or even a birder to identify this as an owl. That's because a lot of basic taxonomy is part of the being-a-human package. The twelve-step program includes things that many people know and often take for granted, and shows how they can be used to help you identify birds.

A quick look might make some birders think Long-eared Owl—the slim build, rusty face, and upright ear tufts; but a second look confirms Great Horned—note the barred underparts and lack of a black vertical band through the eyes. *Baja California Sur, Mexico, 15 October 2015.*

5

While there is evolutionary value to distinguishing a bird you can eat (a duck) from one that might steal your food (a crow), there's little impetus for distinguishing small, drab songbirds. If Gray Flycatcher were poisonous, but Dusky Flycatcher delicious, then humans would likely have been able to tell them apart well before 1939, when Dusky was formally recognized as a "new" species, distinct from Gray Flycatcher (shown here). *Baja California Sur, Mexico, 11 December 2015.*

finding such a rare bird was easy. It made several passes, but always just beyond the brightness of the lights. Then, as Steve was leaving, it landed in a tree—by hanging upside down by its feet! It was a large fruit bat, not an owl . . . oops.

Another time, an experienced birder sent Steve photos of "an unusual hummingbird" from Mexico. Steve puzzled for a while, and then realized it was a large hawk moth! His friend was a little chagrined with the reply: "Are you sure it's a bird? Did you count the spiracles?" But the point here is that in order to identify a bird to species, it first needs to be a bird. You can't get there from here if you're trying to turn a sphinx moth into a hummingbird, a fruit bat into an owl, or a white piece of trash on a distant fence into a Gyrfalcon.

Step 1, then, is taxonomy, the fundamental basis to birding. Taxonomy is simply a fancy word for the organization and naming of things—in this case, birds. Whether or not you realize it, taxonomy is part of our everyday life, such as telling apples from oranges at the store, or when you go to get your daughter a puppy for her birthday and you don't buy a kitten by mistake. This is basic taxonomy—so you're a taxonomist and you didn't even know it. Despite this, when many birders hear the word *taxonomy* they think of some highbrow, academic subject that is beyond their comprehension, maybe even of secret sects with passwords such as *reciprocal monophyly,* whose members go around celebrating sympatrics day.

If you ask any group of birders about taxonomy, the questions can come thick and fast: Why does it keep changing? Why is this considered a species but not that? Can taxonomy help me as a birder? Why is it all so confusing? Who makes the decisions? Why should I care? While we can't promise to answer all of these questions to your satisfaction, we hope we can demystify taxonomy a little and explain how it can be your friend—and help to make birding easier and more fun.

HIGHER-LEVEL TAXONOMY: AMONG FAMILIES

Taxonomy works on the principle of relatedness, and closely related species are grouped together into various categories. For birders, the most familiar categories are *genus* (plural *genera*) and *family*. A genus is a group of closely related species, and a family is a grouping of genera and species. If a genus contains only one species it is termed a *monotypic* genus (literally, "of one type"), indicating the species has no very close living relatives. Examples include Limpkin (also a monotypic family) and Ivory Gull.

Traditionally, taxonomy has relied on the comparison of museum specimens, mainly using structural and plumage features to divine

Since time immemorial, falcons and hawks have been linked in human perception as "birds of prey," or raptors, for their predatory behavior. As a consequence, they have been placed next to each other in taxonomic lists and field guides. Genetic studies, however, indicate that falcons share a common ancestor with parrots. Thus, some lists and even some field guides now put falcons (such as this juvenile Peregrine) next to parrots, and just before songbirds. While this relationship is interesting, it's not knowledge that helps readily with field identification. Who knows, perhaps someday this Peregrine Falcon may even be renamed "Cosmopolitan Death Parrot." *Monterey County, California, 29 July 2014.*

relationships. Big birds and waterbirds were traditionally placed at the start of the list, and smaller birds and colorful songbirds last. It was a convenient way to organize things, and it made some sort of organic sense.

The traditional sequence of families lasted for many years, right through the birth of birding and of modern field guides, most of which were arranged more or less in taxonomic sequence. With time, factors such as voice, habitat, and behavior were incorporated into taxonomic studies, but the sequence of bird families remained largely unchanged. From the 1950s through the 1980s, and even into the 1990s, birders could pick up a field guide for any part of the world and find their way around without much problem. So far, so good.

But then along came genetics. One of the results of the constant fiddling that characterizes the human species has been a new appreciation of genes, and how they might help us more accurately infer how living things are related. In a perfect world, genetics could tell us how closely related Family A is to Family B, when Family C diverged from Family D, and so on. Although the world isn't perfect, genetic analyses have nonetheless helped us to better understand how bird families are related, and to which family most species belong.

Not surprisingly, as more studies are conducted, some of our traditional ideas about relationships are being challenged and overturned. For example, now we are told that parrots share a common ancestor with falcons, grebes with flamingos, and so on. This may seem shocking at first, largely because our nice, ordered world has been shuffled around, but it isn't that crazy. Under different conditions, birds with the same ancestor will change in response to their environment—such as all the Galapagos finches (which genetics now tell us are tanagers!) evolving to fill different roles in the brave new world colonized by their ancestors.

Largely as a result of recent genetic studies, there has been wholesale reordering of bird families in many books, as humans strive to keep up with the latest versions of taxonomy. No two field guides follow the same sequence, because each one adopts new findings, which are appearing at an exponential rate. What many people fail to recognize, however, is that birds evolve in three dimensions of space across a fourth dimension, time. It is inherently impossible to produce a linear sequence of families, let alone species, yet all taxonomic checklists and field guides do just that, conveniently sidestepping or ignoring the "impossible" bit.

Ironically perhaps, the only North American field guides to birds that exactly followed taxonomic sequence were the first Peterson Field Guides. In those days there weren't masses of birders, and plates with facing text were not financially viable. But while Peterson's text followed taxonomic sequence, the plates (scattered throughout the book) did not. Instead, they grouped similar species together, such as Plate 54, "Birds of Fields, Prairies, Plains," from the second edition of *Field Guide to Western Birds,* which featured meadowlarks, longspurs, larks, pipits, Dickcissel, Bobolink, and Lark Bunting. This is a logical, field-friendly grouping of potentially similar birds that might be found in the same habitat.

The purpose of field guides is to enable users to identify birds they see *in the field,* not in the genetics lab, and most users are not taxonomists. If writers of field guides wish to serve their constituency, it

A field guide intended to help the user identify birds in the field might put vireos (such as this Philadelphia Vireo) near other small, superficially similar arboreal birds, such as warblers. Taxonomically, however, these families are not closely related, so you can now find vireos near crows and jays in some field guides. *Baja California, Mexico, 17 October 2015.*

might make sense to adopt and maintain a helpful and somewhat logical sequence, like the simple but brilliant one Roger Tory Peterson used years ago. Instead, many authors shift families willy-nilly with each edition and each new book.

It will be years before taxonomists agree on the sequence of bird families, let alone which species go where. Yet vireos and warblers will always share superficial similarities that make it helpful to group them together in a field guide. Sure, it's interesting to know that vireos and crows are more closely related than are vireos and warblers, but does it help us with field identification? Not so much.

MID-LEVEL TAXONOMY: WITHIN FAMILIES AND GENERA

While the *sequence* of bird families doesn't necessarily help you as a birder, the shared characteristic of birds *within a family* (or within a genus) can be very helpful, be they structural, behavioral, or even vocal. All wrens have barred wings and tails; swifts don't perch on wires but swallows do; curlews (genus *Numenius*) are large sandpipers with decurved bills, whereas godwits (genus *Limosa*) are large sandpipers with ever-so-slightly upturned bills; longspurs are dirt-huggers that scurry low to the ground, but often fly strongly when flushed; most sparrows hop, and don't fly far when flushed, and so on.

An early birding memory for Steve was checking the wintering Reed Buntings at his garden bird feeder for a Lapland Bunting (as Lapland Longspur is called in Britain). The field guide pointed to some differences in wing pattern and face pattern, but failed to mention the very different habits of these different genera (now different families): Lapland Bunting wouldn't visit a bird feeder in a small suburban garden!

For most people, it's easier to learn the characters of fifty basic units (say, bird families) rather than of five hundred scattered units (say, bird species). When you start birding, try to avoid the urge to simply identify a species and move on. Notice what genus it's in (the first part of the scientific name, as in *Melospiza* for *Melospiza melodia,* the Song Sparrow), see what other species are in that genus (in this case, Lincoln's and Swamp Sparrows), and see if you can find shared characters that might help you the next time you see a sparrow.

As a birder, you soon learn that common names don't necessarily indicate relatedness—think Snow Bunting, Lark Bunting, and Indigo Bunting, all in different families. But Snow Bunting is in the same family as longspurs, with which it shares numerous behavioral and even vocal characteristics.

LOWER-LEVEL TAXONOMY: THE SPECIES

The species is the basic currency of birding. Once you have identified a bird to species, a whole world is opened up that would otherwise be unavailable without having a formal name. And not just for birding. Bird conservation, studies of ecology, of biodiversity, and so on are all built upon the premise of birds being identified to species.

But what is a species? Ornithology is full of debates about this question, but don't worry, we're not going to ramble on about the merits of one species concept over another; those of you with a deeper interest can wade into that quagmire in your own time. If there were a simple answer, somebody would have found it by now, which should tell you something.

Still, regardless of all the debate over species concepts, there is general agreement that "species" exist. The important word to note here, however, is not species but *concept,* a word that so many seem to forget in their heated discussions about the biological species concept versus the phylogenetic species concept, and so on. All our ideas about what constitutes a species are just that—ideas, or concepts. They help us to manage and make sense of the world around us.

Although genetic analyses have greatly helped reshape our understanding of higher-level taxonomy, they have to date been less helpful at the levels of genus and species. Basically, "Avian geneticists are still

This female Indigo Bunting might look like just another "little brown bird." However, as with other members of its genus, *Passerina*, it often switches its tail side to side, a behavioral feature that can quickly eliminate a number of other little brown birds from consideration. This is simply one way an appreciation of taxonomy can help you in the field. *Galveston County, Texas, 26 April 2013.*

groping around in a recently tilled but dimly lit field, learning how to use their new tools."[1] The dance won't be over until the music stops, and when it comes to species-level and even genus-level taxonomy, it seems we have little more than a vague idea of the molecular beat.

Despite this, some people blindly view genetics as the be-all and end-all. They don't seem to realize that even with credible genetic studies, it's *still* subjective. Lines are being drawn on a continuum of evolution, no matter what criteria you choose to examine. Like so many things in life, it simply comes down to a matter of opinion.[2]

If you as a birder find it all rather arbitrary, you may find solace in the fact that, well, it *is* arbitrary. Anyone can read the evidence and make his or her own decisions. However, birders seeking common ground to communicate find it helpful to adopt a standardized list of species. To this end, the American Birding Association (ABA) follows the opinions of the American Ornithological Society (AOS), as published in their *Checklist of North and Middle American Birds*.[3] For better or worse, the AOS committee tasked with keeping the list requires data to be published before they act, even if different species are staring them in the face.

Examples of candidates for separate species that are staring us in the face, but which are not (yet) split by the AOS—even if data have been published and other taxonomic authorities treat some of these as species—include eastern and western Warbling Vireos, eastern and western Marsh Wrens, Myrtle and Audubon's Warblers, and the various members of the Herring Gull complex, Northern Pygmy-Owl complex, and Fox Sparrow complex. There are plenty more, and that's only in North America.

Not surprisingly, some ornithologists have suggested we need a paradigm shift.[4] Their argument is that if a lot of data (formally unpublished perhaps, but often readily accessible to anyone) point to a split, then go ahead and split, rather than wait years for some grad student to write a thesis and painfully elaborate the obvious. If others disagree with the split, the burden of proof should be on them to disprove it, not the other way around. This approach has obvious appeal, as well as merit, and it may be the way of the future. But that's just our opinion.

SHOULD YOU CARE?

Let's revisit the earlier questions we've heard from birders, and offer quick answers distilled from the preceding paragraphs.

Q: *Why does taxonomy keep changing?*
A: Human nature, our constant quest to learn. This doesn't mean that field guide sequence needs to keep changing: field guides and taxonomic lists are two different things, like church and state.

Bewick's Swan is a good example of the arbitrary nature of species-level taxonomy. Long considered a distinct species, Bewick's is now usually lumped with Whistling Swan, the combined species being known as Tundra Swan. However, no critical study has been made of this matter, and even first-year birds can be distinguished in the field by bill pattern (note the extensive pale pink bill base on this young Bewick's). An equally defensible approach would be to treat Bewick's as a separate species, pending critical study. *Marin County, California, 18 November 2014.*

Q: *Why is this considered a species but not that?*
A: Simply a matter of opinion. Species are useful handles.

Q: *Can taxonomy help me as a birder?*
A: Absolutely. Learning the characteristics of families and genera is a great way to speed up your learning and improve your birding.

WHO "THEY" ARE . . .

In North America, when birders say things such as "Where did they put longspurs?" the "they" usually refers to the North American Classification Committee (NACC) of the American Ornithological Society (or AOS; formerly the AOU, or American Ornithologists' Union). The AOS is simply a club of ornithologists, and like many clubs it has various committees. The NACC's job is to maintain a checklist of all birds recorded in North America. "They" therefore move families and species around, decide which species are formally recognized, and so on.

The American Birding Association (ABA) and eBird follow the AOS checklist mainly for convenience and political reasons, rather than any endorsement of merit. In other parts of the world, other self-elected bodies fulfill parallel roles, and there is an international body (the International Ornithological Union) that maintains and evaluates a world checklist.[5] Birders who keep lists can choose one of several lists to follow, although it's a bit like different religions. The thinking person realizes sooner or later that these different checklists, or species concepts, can't all be right, but often there's some comfort, or convenience, in following one or the other.

Q: *Why is it all so confusing?*
A: That's life, and if you're not confused, then clearly you don't understand what's going on.

Q: *Who makes the decisions?*
A: That depends. There are several taxonomic authorities out there; the ABA, at least for now, follows the AOS. You're also perfectly

capable of making your own decisions, but it takes time, and most people let others do this for them.

Q: *Why should I care?*

A: You don't need to care at all, and you may even be happier that way. But we hope we've provided some background that might swing you toward caring a little, or at least being curious about how the birds you see are related to one another—and how that can help you identify them.

The bottom line: higher-level taxonomy is usually unhelpful for birding. Species-level taxonomy is a matter of opinion. But in between, at the levels of family and genus, that's where taxonomy can be really helpful for birding. So now that we know we're looking at a bird, and that calling it a species is simply an opinion, what's our next step?

Why Is Birding Like Selling Real Estate? (Location)

E arly in this project we asked several people: "What's the single most important thing when identifying a bird?" Nobody came up with the answer right away, a few people did after some wrong guesses and clues, but many never got it. And of course, it's just our opinion what's most important, and this all assumes you're looking at a bird (see Step 1).

Step 2 is a key factor in identifying birds, and pretty much anyone you ask, birder or non-birder, knows the answer. Together with Steps 3 and 4 it forms "the big three," the underlying base that experienced birders often take for granted and beginners perhaps don't pay enough attention to.

OPPOSITE: Many people don't give Great Blue Heron much of a second glance, which is a pity because it's a big, beautiful bird. It's well known to birders and many non-birders alike, and basically it's the only large gray heron you're ever likely to see in North America. Then again, the bird shown here is a Gray Heron, the Old World counterpart, which differs from Great Blue in a number of ways, none of which is likely to strike most people at a glance. *Somerset, England, 11 May 2015.*

WHERE IS THE ANSWER

Let's think about it from the point of view of using a field guide, something most of us were never taught to do—we just picked up the book and started using it. You see an unfamiliar bird, or at least a bird you don't immediately recognize. You open a field guide and there's so much choice—hundreds of species, some with different plumages for males, females, juveniles, even different seasonal plumages. It can seem overwhelming, and, okay, it will take a bit of work (investment might be a better word) to find your way around a field guide. But hidden in plain sight is something so basic that most birders don't realize how important it is.

So what does a field guide have? *Pictures!* Yes, it does, but that's not it. *Text?* Yes, that too, but what else? *Oh, maps?* Correct. Put another way: Why is selling real estate like identifying birds? Because the single most important thing is . . . location. Are there Boreal Chickadees in California? Black-capped Chickadees in Florida? Carolina Chickadees in Alaska? What's so funny about rhetorical questions? Location can be a continent, a state, a county, even one side of a river and not the other.

While coarse scale distribution is covered by field guide maps, local distribution can also be very helpful. Many parks or refuges have bird checklists, and most states and provinces, even some counties, have published works that cover the status and distribution of their birdlife, such as breeding bird atlases. For the more serious birder, the journal *North American Birds*[1] offers an overview of bird distribution across the continent, often with essays that synthesize and illuminate patterns.

Like any aspect of birding, to learn the nuances of your local bird distribution would take some work, that four-letter word we so often run from. But if that work is not for you, don't worry—these days it's easy to go online and pull up a map of any species' distribution in seconds, tailored to your state, county, or even a specific birding location, as with eBird,[2] which is discussed more fully in Step 12.

Red-tailed Hawk is one of the commonest and most widespread birds in North America. It has notoriously variable plumage, but nice adults like this with a red tail are pretty distinctive, no? You can even see the dark patagial mark (leading edge to the underwing) that all the field guides tell you is diagnostic. Oh, but these are Rufous-tailed Hawks, from South America. Location, location, location. Why isn't Rufous-tailed Hawk an isolated race of Red-tailed Hawk? From Step 1 you know the answer—it's simply an opinion. *Araucanía, Chile, 24 October 2015.*

ASSUMPTIONS MAKE LIFE EASIER

A big part of bird distribution is linked to the assumptions we make every time we go birding. We assume the crows we see in California are American Crows, not Northwestern Crows or Fish Crows, that the meadowlarks we see in Maine are Eastern Meadowlarks, and so on. But do we really check every single crow and meadowlark carefully? Should we? When watching birds, remember that most of what you see fits into what is known about the birds in your area, and the maps in your field guides are like gold.

Starting with assumptions makes things manageable, but don't completely kiss your assumptions goodbye. As you become more experienced and observant, you will probably find things that are "rare" in a given location, or at a given season, so it's good to keep an open mind. It's helpful, though, to know the difference between an open mind and one unconstrained by reality—it has been said that some birders need imagination-stabilizing binoculars! Those are the people who clearly have never learned to look at the maps in field guides. As they say, if you hear the sound of hooves, think zebras—but only if you're in the Serengeti.

RARE BIRDS

It's a human trait to focus on exceptions, and some people like to say, "Birds have wings and can use them." However, that's a bit like saying "The British have taste buds . . ." Here we will mention in passing "rare birds"—birds that turn up where or when they "shouldn't," birds that garner a disproportionate amount of attention among some birders. There's a whole book devoted to rare birds of California, and of North America, but no comparable books for the common birds. There are rare birds committees but no common birds committees.

The bottom line is that rare birds are, well, rare, and while the chances of your finding one are slightly better than of winning the lottery, most species have well-defined and well-documented distributions. Thus, anything you think you see outside of a mapped field guide range should be carefully evaluated, because at least 999 times out of 1,000, when it comes to range the bird is right. When using a field guide, first try to match the picture with what you saw, *then check the map*.

It's good to accept early on that some birds will get away as unidentified. Probably they were just common species not seen well enough; both of us frequently see birds we just have to let go, and perhaps some

Everything is rare somewhere. In Europe, birders would be flocking by the thousands to see this rather drab Willet (the right-hand, back bird), but in the United States, the Marsh Sandpiper in the foreground would have the same effect. This was the first Marsh Sandpiper found in North America outside of Alaska, and quite an exciting moment for the finders! *Baja California, Mexico, 12 October 2011.*

of them were rarities. Sometimes, though, a second look, a nagging thought, or, most importantly, another opinion can help resolve the matter—and you may have found a rare bird.

For example, on finding the first Greater Sand Plover in North America, which was at first sleeping and then awoke to show its bill, the observers thought something like "Snowy Plover? Not a Snowy . . . Oh, big bill—Wilson's Plover? No, wait—huh, must be a Lesser Sand Plover, but, hmm, big bill . . . Greater? No, it can't be, here in California?"

Oh no, it's one of "those" flycatchers, in the genus *Empidonax* (Empi-don't-ask?). At least it's one of the green ones with a yellowish throat, which cuts our choices greatly. And where was it? In southernmost Mexico. Oh, so it's a Yellowish Flycatcher, a nonmigratory species unrecorded in the United States, but not readily separable by sight in the field (or in a photo) from Cordilleran and Pacific-slope Flycatchers. Might Yellowish Flycatcher have been over-looked in the United States? Probably not. Whether you like it or not, probability is an inherent part of birding. *Chiapas, Mexico, 2 March 2007.*

(Greater Sand Plover nests in interior Central and East Asia, and winters from Africa east to Australia.)

Distinguishing these two species (Lesser and Greater) isn't so easy, especially if you're not that familiar with them, and especially if one of them isn't even known to occur in your hemisphere and therefore isn't in the field guide. The bird was left for weeks as "unidentified sand plover, suspected Greater" (remember, there's no penalty for not identifying a bird), until it was caught, measured, and its identity confirmed as Greater. In hindsight, the ID was fairly straightforward, but that's what hindsight is for. Identifying the second Greater Sand Plover found in North America was much easier, because the dam of expectations had been breached.

By knowing it's a bird (and roughly what kind of bird) and knowing where you are, you've already taken two big steps. It wasn't that hard, was it? Now for Step 3, also an easy one.

STEP 3

Are Your Feet Wet? (Habitat)

S o now you know where you are, and you're looking at a bird, not a moth or a flying fish. What's another important, but obvious, thing to consider? A clue: you wouldn't look for a White-tailed Tropicbird on alpine tundra anymore than you'd look for a White-tailed Ptarmigan offshore on a pelagic trip. Clearly these are extremes, but habitat, Step 3, is a very important part of birding.

The good news is that by simply looking around a place you usually have a pretty good idea of the general habitat you're in, without needing to be an expert botanist or geologist. Are you in a conifer forest or an open grassland, in a marshy wetland or on a sandy beach? Recognizing even coarse habitat differences really helps in understanding what birds you might expect to encounter. Experience is the best way to gain knowledge about subtler habitat clues, but good field guides should at least key you into the broader habitat categories.

OPPOSITE: Birding from the bow of a boat, well offshore in the deep blue waters of the Gulf Stream, would be a poor choice if you were seeking desert land birds such as Verdin and Greater Roadrunner. But if you're hoping to see Black-capped Petrel and Band-rumped Storm-Petrel, which favor this oceanic desert, then you'd be in the right habitat. A big part of birding involves the recognition of habitats at all scales, which can help you identify birds as well as find them. *Dare County, North Carolina, 5 June 2010.*

Many bird names give clues about their habitat. For example, even on migration the Rock Wren seeks out barren rocky and stony situations; seeing one in a woodland would be exceptional, to put it mildly. *Marin County, California, 22 September 2015.*

CONTEXT, FROM CONTINENT TO COUNTY

The degree to which habitat can help with bird ID varies with location, and also sometimes with season—but that's Step 4, so let's not get ahead of ourselves. And, as with so many things in birding, habitat is simply a clue. Still, it's an important one, and it seems to be one that many people forget about. "I saw this brown bird, it had X, Y, and Z . . ." Well, what habitat was it in? We see so much but observe so little; trying to be aware of habitat is a good skill to build. Some examples of habitat differences are easily appreciated and widely applicable; others are subtler.

Across most of North America, if you see some small white egrets wading out in a wetland, there's a very high probability they are Snowy Egrets. If you see a group of small white egrets in a dry field, away from water, they're likely Cattle Egrets, especially if they're around livestock. If you've never seen either species before, you'll want to confirm the ID with other features, but habitat would be a big first clue. A Sharp-shinned Hawk or Cooper's Hawk sitting out in the open on a fencepost along the edge of a field is very likely a Cooper's, not the shade-loving Sharp-shinned, which tends to stay within cover. But Cooper's also often perches in cover, so this is a one-way clue.

Simply by careful observation, you may discover habitat clues that help you with local birding. In the counties where we live, in central California, Swainson's Thrush nests mainly in riparian deciduous woods with appreciable understory, whereas Hermit Thrush nests mainly in conifer woods with a more open understory. In fact, you could walk along in spring with your eyes closed and predict the habitat by which species of thrush is singing.

It's also fun to learn which species share habitats. For example, along with Swainson's Thrushes there are usually Wilson's Warblers and Song Sparrows, which like shady, moist, and rather dense understory. Along with Hermit Thrushes there are usually Golden-crowned Kinglets and Brown Creepers, which also favor tall, conifer-dominated forest.

After a while, you might be able to look at an area and make a good guess as to what suite of bird species you could expect to find there. On the other hand, when a species is absent from a seemingly suitable habitat, you might wonder why that is—and in the process learn more about the habitat requirements of your common neighborhood birds. It's an easy and fun exercise that you can practice anywhere.

LOCATION AND HABITAT COMBINED

Although habitat is rarely infallible, it can be very helpful, if for no other reason than to eliminate species from consideration. Combining habitat and location, we can further limit the possibilities, which is what ID is all about—narrowing your choice until only one possibility is left standing. If your bird is not only in the "wrong" place but also in the "wrong" habitat for the species you're considering, that's two strikes against it, and chances are it is something else.

Therefore, before you get bogged down in details of plumage, structure, and so on, step back and ask yourself the questions: Where am I and what is the habitat? If you're thinking, "I know Nuttall's Woodpecker isn't supposed to be here, but the face pattern doesn't look quite right for Ladder-backed, and, well . . ." Before going too far down what may be the wrong road, ask yourself: Am I in oak woodland or desert scrub? There are a few places where these species could overlap in range, but they still tend to segregate by habitat.

Perusing images online shows how non-birding photographers often ignore or overlook clues such as habitat and location. One of our favorites is a "male Smith's Longspur" perched up in an oak tree, which would be a highly unusual place for Smith's Longspur, normally a bird of wild open spaces. But it would be a typical place to find a female Black-headed Grosbeak, which shares some similarities in overall plumage coloration and pattern with a male Smith's Longspur. Experienced birders might never consider these species similar. Yet simply trying to match a photo to a picture in a field guide, without taking

Most people associate ducks with water, but "water" comprises many different habitats. If you wanted to see a Wood Duck, here a male, you'd be better off looking in wooded freshwater wetlands, perhaps even up in the trees themselves, rather than out on open water or on salt water. *Grand Forks County, North Dakota, 2 June 2016.*

into account context such as habitat and location, could lead you to this misidentification.

The pictures in your field guides should be helpful, and the maps are very helpful, but don't ignore the text. A few well-chosen words about habitat can be extremely useful.

STEP 4

Well-Seasoned
Assumptions (Season)

From the preceding steps, we know where we are, and we have some idea of the habitat. There's one more very basic thing to consider when identifying birds, and again it's something anyone on the street could tell you. Step 4, the last of "the big three," is date, or at least season, which is often linked to location and, to a lesser degree, to habitat.

The great thing about this is that even somebody who started birding yesterday knows where they are, the date, and to some degree the habitat they're in: a coastal river mouth in Oregon in September, the Gulf Stream off North Carolina in June, a conifer forest in Ontario in December, a reservoir in interior Texas in April. We all have this information. The important thing is how we use it—or, all too often, *don't* use it.

OPPOSITE: Knowing location and habitat isn't always enough to find a bird. You need to be in the right place at the right time. To see an Atlantic Puffin in North America, your best bet is in Atlantic Canada or New England. However, you almost certainly wouldn't see any there if you went in December, when puffins are wintering far out at sea in the North Atlantic. They start to return to their colonies in April, but you're better off waiting until late May or June just to be sure. *Skomer Island, Wales, 8 May 2015.*

(Or, as the sign in the window for the spring sale at the camping store said: "Now is the discount of our winter tent.") In large part because of cold winters (or, conversely, hot summers), many bird species in North America are migratory: as a rule, birds here usually fly north in summer to breed, south in winter to find areas with more food. In a global sense, however, most bird species are not migratory, so you could find them in their range and habitat throughout the year.

This means, for example, that in June you can find Spruce Grouse and Blackpoll Warblers in the same wooded park in Anchorage, Alaska, but in January, while the grouse is still there, the Blackpoll Warblers should be contentedly in the warmer climes of South America. These are obviously extremes, between which lie an almost infinite number of combinations for different species in different parts of the continent.

Just as there are degrees of geographic scale, there are degrees of seasonality, which are often linked to geography. For example, if you see a thrush with a spotted breast (genus *Catharus*) anywhere in the United States in midwinter, you can pretty safely assume it's a Hermit Thrush, not a Swainson's Thrush, which winters in tropical regions south of the United States. (Okay, so there are a few midwinter records of Swainson's Thrush north of Mexico, but there are more winter records of Rustic Bunting, a vagrant from Asia, which should put things into context.) However, if you see a spot-breasted thrush in mid- to late May in Central Park, New York, it's likely not to be a Hermit Thrush, as most have migrated north by then, and a Swainson's Thrush is more likely at that time.

Often there are timing differences between eastern and western North America. For example, in spring, migrant Common Nighthawks appear in Florida and south Texas by April but rarely before late May in California.

As with birding by habitat, after a while you'll be able to make predictions based on season. The swallows of San Juan Capistrano are a

As with Atlantic Puffin, if you want to see Kumlien's Gull (aka Iceland Gull, depending on your taxonomy) in North America, your best bet is Atlantic Canada or New England. However, the wrong time for puffins would be the right time for Kumlien's Gulls. These Arctic breeders start migrating south in October, but not before November do many reach the Northeast, and you're better off waiting until December or January if you want to be pretty sure of finding some. *Newfoundland, Canada, 5 February 2002.*

famous example, but anywhere you watch birds you'll start to detect patterns for any number of species. For example, in fifteen years of watching birds at a pond in the town where he lives, Steve has seen Blue-winged Teal only three times in spring: a pair on 19 May 2003, a male on 20 May 2012, and a female on 18 May 2015. The three spring records of Spotted Sandpiper on the same pond fall on 14 May 2002, 13 May 2008, and 12 May 2009. The coincidence of dates is remarkable (and there are other examples), but birds are creatures of habit, their migrations honed over thousands of years of adaptation to climate.

In days gone by, encyclopedic knowledge of status and distribution was the preserve of a few souls with access to good libraries and lots of

Buff-breasted Sandpipers breed on remote Arctic tundra and winter in southern South America. Not surprisingly, then, birders in North America most often see this attractive species during its spring or fall migrations. If you live on the West Coast, your best chance of finding a "Buffy" would be from late August through September, when small numbers of juveniles usually pass through. *Marin County, California, 29 August 2008.*

reading time, but today anyone can access this information in minutes. For example, with eBird,[1] a free online database, you can pull up seasonal bar charts for birds in locations as large as a state or as small as your own backyard. These visual displays of real data help you quickly get a sense of what species to expect in a place at a given time of year. To learn all of these combinations and permutations would take many lifetimes, but simply being aware of seasonal patterns—remember the different colors on the range maps in your field guide—is the important thing to learn.

THREE STRIKES AND YOU'RE OUT

Knowing seasonal patterns, in concert with distribution and habitat, also limits your possibilities and can lead to quicker ID in the field. There may be almost fifty species of sparrows in North America (help!), but not all of them occur in your area, in grassy fields, in July, and so on.

Let's say you're following a hawk along a wooded stream in coastal

California, and you think it may be a juvenile Swainson's Hawk, perhaps because the head looks whitish overall. Although it's possible you have a juvenile Swainson's Hawk, that species is a rare migrant in the area, and it's typically a bird of open country—perching out in fields, often on the ground. Given these two strikes, an experienced birder would consider an unusually pale-headed Red-shouldered Hawk or a young Cooper's Hawk as more likely options. Looking at other features could confirm the ID, but habitat together with location suggest that a conclusion based solely on a plumage-related field mark might be wrong. And if the date were, say, early January, then you have three strikes against the ID (almost all Swainson's Hawks winter to the south of the United States). This still doesn't mean it isn't a Swainson's Hawk, but it would be very, very unlikely. You'd want to carefully document such an unusual occurrence—unusual in location, in habitat, and in season.

Sometimes, just sometimes, your reasonable assumptions prove wrong. Any "pumpkin-faced" sparrow in California in winter is rare. The default option is Nelson's Sparrow, which this bird was initially thought to be. A second opinion, however, identified it as Le Conte's Sparrow, the first ever found wintering in central California. *Marin County, California, 26 December 2014.*

Ever ask an experienced birder or field trip leader how they knew a bird was species X? They usually fill in with "It had this plumage feature and this structural feature, and . . . ," none of which you saw—and, in truth, little or none of which they saw. Yes, the species in question has those field marks, but that's not really what was used to ID it. They might as well say it has a violet-striped intestine and lays four creamy eggs speckled with ochraceous buff.

Being honest, they might say: "It's mid-July in Kentucky, in a short-grass field, and that's the only species here that is vaguely like this, at this season, in this habitat." Yet we see experienced birders all the time say things like "It was streaked on the cheeks and had a yellow patch on the lesser wing coverts . . ." We call foul, or male bovine feces. All they saw was a brief glimpse of shape and color, and their mind filled in the rest *based on assumptions grounded in knowledge and preconceptions*. More than 99 percent of the time those assumptions will prove to be right, but does that make such people good birders or simply lazy birders?

A plea to more experienced birders: please be honest if you wish to help less experienced birders. Try to explain *what you really saw, what clues you used*, not what characteristics you know the bird had. In doing this, you may even become a better birder. Try it next time and see how much more you might learn, even if it's only to acknowledge how big a role assumptions play in your daily birding or, for that matter, in life.

START AT THE BEGINNING

So many beginning birding classes seem to start with things like "Let's look at the structure of the bill." Yes, structure can be important, but a real bird doesn't exist simply as an image on the screen. A bird is the embodiment of context, so much more than simply the sum of its parts. If you're looking at a bird in life, then you know where you are, the date, and what kind of habitat you're in. Sometimes location and habitat are enough, but in other cases, as they say, timing is everything.

We suspect that half or more of the regularly occurring bird species

Buller's Shearwater is a regular migrant off the West Coast, but seeing one is a combination of luck (as with most ocean birding) and timing. In some years thousands are seen, in other years just a few tens. You might be lucky and see one in August, but the main window of occurrence is from mid-September to mid-October. *Marin County, California, 25 October 2010.*

in North America could be identified to species by just a basic knowledge of birds (duck versus owl versus sparrowlike), quick perusal of a field guide, and *an appreciation of location, habitat, and season.*

STEP 5

Can You See the Light? (Lighting)

O wls and some other birds (more than you might think, perhaps) are active at night, but most birds sleep when it's dark, as do humans, at least traditionally—for the very simple reason that it's difficult to see in the dark. If you need to see food, or predators, then adequate light is critical. But while daylight allows us to see birds easily, variation in its quality can also play plenty of tricks on the human eye and mind.

Steps 1 through 4 covered the fundamentals. Things like location, habitat, and season are pretty much fixed while you're looking at a bird. So now we'll look at a couple of external factors that can change as we watch a bird and affect what we perceive—factors over which we often have little or no control. The first of these is Step 5, lighting, or rather, an appreciation of how different lighting can affect what we see, or think we see. Despite the inherent importance of light to watching birds, most birders don't think much about it, other than moving to get a bird in good light or standing so the sun isn't in their eyes.

OPPOSITE: Hummingbirds are one of the best examples of how even a slight change in lighting can dramatically affect a bird's appearance. One second, the "helmet" of this male Costa's Hummingbird may appear blackish; the next second, it flashes a dazzling array of purples and blues. *Monterey County, California, 2 May 2015.*

Here are the four compass points viewed from a boat, in the same minute. The sea looks very different in each direction, and it follows that the appearance

of any bird viewed under these different lighting conditions could also vary. *Sonoma County, California, 30 September 2012.*

Experienced birders assimilate lighting into any ID equation (or they should), but when starting out it's easy to be fooled. For example, what color is a crow? Well, black, obviously. Yet in bright sun, a coal-black crow can reflect silvery and look far from black. In low light, blues in particular can appear duller, more grayish. And in bright sun, white areas can easily be "burned out" at the expense of adjacent colors and patterns. Every fall, on a sunny pelagic trip off California, we see eager observers, even trip leaders sometimes, call out "Buller's Shearwater!" But the bird is simply a Pink-footed Shearwater in bright, low-angle sunlight, which makes the dusky underparts appear gleaming white and heightens contrast between the dark head and white throat.

Those poor souls who pore over flocks of gulls soon learn that even a slight difference in the angle of light relative to a standing gull can produce an appreciable difference in the apparent gray tone of a gull's upperparts. Thus, two adult gulls of the same species can show appreciably different gray tones simply because of their angle to the sun. Not as drastic as the changes you see with hummingbird gorgets, but far more likely to lead you astray in terms of identification. Indeed, we know some larophiles (birders obsessed with gulls) who don't even leave the house if it's sunny—they prefer to wait for a slightly cloudy day, when they can more readily appreciate veritable shades of gray.

If you need another reason to "not do gulls," birds standing on ice and snow often appear darker-backed than they really are, thanks to reflected light. Consequently, for example, in parts of Alaska it's easy to mistake the local, relatively dark-backed "Herring Gull" (actually a distinct species, Vega Gull—at least, that's one opinion) for the even darker-backed Slaty-backed Gull.

Tricks of the light can fool all of us at some time or another. If you think you see something unusual, consider whether lighting might play a role in your perceptions. Is it late in the day, when golden sunlight changes colors and makes things appear warmer than usual? Is the gull in question standing at a different angle to the others? Is a bird backlit, so

Quick, how many species of gulls in this picture? You might think several, but look carefully and you might conclude, well, only two species—really! This image of fifty adult gulls, each a slightly different shade of gray, includes twenty or so Western Gulls, at least one Glaucous-winged Gull, and, okay, so we cheated a bit, a good number of hybrids between Western and Glaucous-winged, which in some areas of the West Coast can outnumber the parent species.

Although some shades of gray here are thanks to the hybrids, a lot of the variation in gray tones is simply because different birds are resting at slightly different angles relative to the light. *Marin County, California, 23 December 2015.*

that perhaps you can't see the traditional field marks? Does it really have white outer tail feathers, or is that just the light shining through them?

Sadly, we can't offer a silver bullet to overcome the vicissitudes of lighting. Just being aware of lighting and how it can vary is the main thing. Perhaps the next time you're out birding, watch the common birds in different lights and notice how their appearance can change. You'll soon start to absorb the spectrum of possibilities.

BELOW: The classic, pale sky blue of a "field guide" male Mountain Bluebird (as viewed in sunlight, left) can appear a very different blue when viewed in shade or overcast conditions (right), an effect perhaps enhanced in worn versus fresh plumage. *Larimer County, Colorado, 27 July 2016.*

OPPOSITE: The gorgets of adult male hummingbirds are perhaps the most striking examples of how, in a split second, a small shift in the angle of lighting can transform the colors we see. This Broad-tailed Hummingbird was even perched in the shade. Although in field guides the male Broad-tailed has a rose pink gorget, in life the gorget can appear more of a ruby red, as here—depending on the lighting as well as on the freshness of the plumage (see Step 10). *Larimer County, Colorado, 26 July 2016.*

Like most species, Say's Phoebe is not too difficult to identify if seen well at close range and in decent light (left). It's a medium-size, softly toned flycatcher with a cinnamon belly and a contrasting blackish tail. As on many birds, however, light shining through the slightly spread tail can produce the effect of white outer tail feathers (right); this bird is also molting (Step 10), resulting in a strongly forked tail; and it doesn't help that it's not that close (Step 6)—remember, distance is the great deceiver and imagination is the great receiver. *Marin County, California, 30 September 2015 (left); Boulder County, Colorado, 30 July 2016 (right).*

STEP 6

The Great Equalizer (Distance)

Now it's light enough to see and we know it's a bird, plus where we are, the date, and more or less what habitat we're in. Let's step back and look at an equalizing, yet inherently variable, force in birding: distance, which is Step 6. Everyone, absolutely everyone, has a distance at which identification for a given species is not possible.

It's relatively easy to identify a California Condor at over a mile, but a Ruby-throated Hummingbird is invisible at such a distance. And it may be impossible to identify an immature female Rufous or Allen's Hummingbird to species in your hand, even when you can measure the width of its tail feathers. One lesson here, then, is simply that not all birds can be identified correctly to species, but most can, at some distance or other.

A common trait we see among birding guides and field trip leaders is the desire to call out everything they see, regardless of distance. If they're leading an advanced birding group then maybe that's fine, but more often they're not. Most people like to see birds up close, get a good

---

OPPOSITE: California Condor is one of a few species in North America that can be identified without much difficulty from well over a mile away. But even a bird this large can be far enough away that you might be uncertain about the ID. *Baja California, Mexico, 23 June 2015.*

The common and widespread Turkey Vulture (or TV) is a great subject on which to practice identifying birds at a distance. This composite image shows a selection of TVs—and one Golden Eagle. The more time you spend watching TVs, the easier it will be to spot a distant eagle.

view of them, know what they are seeing and why. Distant specks—not so much. Calling out every speck doesn't really help people in the group, especially if the guide is unable to articulate why they believe that some distant dot really is "species A."

The number of hawks we see routinely misidentified at hawk watches is not low, even when experienced hawk watchers are involved. The same is true with jaegers and other species called out on pelagic trips. It's good to remember that although some birders may confidently identify distant specks, a confident identification is not necessarily synonymous with a correct identification. There's nothing wrong with saying, "Hey, this might be a species X" or "Is this perhaps a species Y?"

At close range, an adult Pomarine Jaeger with well-developed tail "spoons" like this is readily identified. But without the spoons, and at anything other than close range, the identification of jaegers becomes fraught with uncertainty. One trick to getting better with distant birds is to keep watching a flying bird until the field marks you used to identify it when close are no longer visible. *Dare County, North Carolina, 27 May 2009.*

If a bird is too far away, it's often best just to let it go and look for something closer. But there is one simple way to get better at identifying distant birds, which is what many of these hawk watchers and pelagic addicts have practiced for innumerable hours. The trick is to watch birds when they're close and you can see clearly what species they are, and then *keep watching them until they are far away*. They're still the same species, and you will know that fact well beyond the range at which any conventional field marks would be visible. If it was an Osprey when it flew right in front of you, it's still an Osprey when it's a mile away—evolution doesn't work that fast.

Having now thought about how a couple of environmental factors can affect what you see in the field, let's look at how a bird interacts with its environment.

OPPOSITE: An adult male Anna's Hummingbird is relatively easy to identify when studied at close range, even if the light isn't revealing the true extent of its iridescent helmet, and especially when you take into account location and season. But at a mile it's probably impossible to even see a hummingbird, let alone identify it to species—unless, perhaps, it's been scaled up for a float in a parade! *Monterey County, California, 1 March 2009 (above); Marin County, California, 4 July 2007 (below).*

STEP 7

What Are You Doing?
(Behavior)

Most birders quickly learn that swifts won't be running around in the grass, or that quail won't be soaring overhead hawking for insects. But again, taking the obvious and refining it is the key, like taxonomy or habitat. Step 7 is the behavior of a species, which may vary with location, season, and even with habitat or a bird's sex. Behavior is so elementary and obvious that many groups of birds are named for it: woodpeckers peck wood, swallows swallow insects, brown creepers creep, shearwaters shear the water, thrashers thrash, cowbirds associate with cattle, and so on. As in most things, though, there are no absolutes, but there are high probabilities.

STEP BACK FROM THE DETAILS

If somebody gave you the following description of a bird they had seen, what would you say? "I was out at Point Reyes, California, the first week

---

OPPOSITE: Jays storing acorns can hammer persistently, and a nuthatch that's found a particularly resonant branch can be pretty noisy, but in general, tapping on a tree usually means a woodpecker. Even more specifically than pecking wood, sapsuckers suck sap, like this Red-breasted Sapsucker. Neat lines of drilled holes on a trunk are a good indication that sapsuckers are, or have been, present. Other birds, such as hummingbirds and warblers, will also feed at the sap wells. *Marin County, California, 27 November 2015.*

---

of September. In the trees near the lighthouse I saw a small flycatcher with a peaked nape, no distinct eye-ring, and pale, but not strongly contrasting, buffy wing-bars. Overall, it was dull olive-brownish above, paler below, with a dusky wash on the chest and a faint yellowish wash on the belly. It had a medium-length bill that was fairly broad, and the lower mandible was pinkish or a sort of yellowish orange, at least at the base; the legs and feet looked blackish. I didn't hear it call."

First, you need to assume it was a flycatcher rather than, say, some kind of vireo, and go from there. It doesn't seem like a bad description, and perhaps this person has taken some classes in bird identification and learned how to describe birds. They even have where, when, and some habitat, and they paid attention to voice, or the lack thereof. But when we look in the field guide, we see a whole suite of flycatchers that could fit this description, so what next?

Well, something very important is missing from this description, something the person surely saw but didn't consciously observe and note down. *What was the flycatcher doing?* Was it perched high on a wire or an open snag, sallying out for insects and returning to its perch? Or was it less conspicuous, lower in the vegetation, making short sallies and often not returning to the same perch? And did it flick its tail up when perched, or just sit still?

When asked about behavior, the person answers "perched high" and "sitting still," which points to a Western Wood Pewee (genus *Contopus*). Had they said "less conspicuous" and "flicking its tail up," that would point to a Willow Flycatcher (genus *Empidonax*). Remember that taxonomy (Step 1) can be your friend—different genera of similar-looking flycatchers can have different behaviors, things that help with field ID.

But also remember how we make assumptions, based on where and when. Two very similar species, Eastern Wood Pewee and Alder Flycatcher, could have been contenders, but both are exceptionally rare in California. More than 99.9 percent of the time the birds you see will be

Western Wood-Pewee (left) and Willow Flycatcher (right) are small flycatchers overall similar in plumage pattern. They can be separated by some structural features, but most of the time they are much more easily distinguished by behavior. *Marin County, California, 18 September 2008 (left); Nayarit, Mexico, 14 January 2016 (right).*

the species that are supposed to be there, so a provisional and probably correct ID in this scenario is Western Wood Pewee. Moreover, the pewee is generally commoner in that area, and more conspicuous than Willow Flycatcher, which adds further support to the probability of the bird's ID as a pewee.

Ultimately, though, you weren't there, and you didn't see the bird, so the best you can do is say, "That sounds like a Western Wood Pewee," explain why, and hope the next time that person comes upon a flycatcher they will pay attention to its behavior, not just its plumage and coloration. In fact, the description they gave was not overly helpful, despite being seemingly quite detailed.

One great thing about behavior is that it's often visible at a much greater distance than are conventional field marks. A small flycatcher

What would you think if we said "We saw a striking bird the other day; it had a bold black-and-white pattern on the wings, and some orange on it some-where. What was it?" Without context, such as habitat and behavior, the description is not very helpful. It could have been a Black-headed Grosbeak, an American Avocet, or a White-tailed Tropicbird, like this. *Dare County, North Carolina, 30 May 2011.*

silhouetted in the mist a hundred yards away sallies out, returns to its high perch, and doesn't flick its tail: it's a pewee, no plumage needed.

SHOREBIRDS—NOT SO HARD, REALLY

Many birders find shorebirds challenging, in part because many species are overall grayish above and whitish below, and in the field guide they can all seem so similar. However, there may be no better example of a group in which behavior helps with ID, especially the manner in which a given species feeds. Perhaps you've seen experienced birders scan a distant marsh or mudflat and identify the various shorebirds out there. Clearly they're not seeing the leg color or even the bill shape, so what are they seeing? Well, most sandpipers have slightly different feeding manners, which reflect their leg length, their bill length, and their bill shape, and these "field marks" can be used at long range.

For example, Stilt Sandpiper, Lesser Yellowlegs, and Wilson's Phalarope are three medium-size sandpipers; they're grayish above and whitish below in nonbreeding plumage; they all have medium-length black bills; they all have fairly long yellowish legs, with feet that project beyond the tail in flight; and they all show white rumps and fairly plain upperwings when they fly off.

While the field guide might point to subtle differences in bill shape, these three species have different feeding behaviors that can be seen at great distance. If the bird is wading out in the water and picking at the surface, it's a Lesser Yellowlegs. If it's wading in the water, probing with

---

As well as what you do see, what you don't see can be important. But what you don't see is, by definition, hard to see. If you watch a Spotted Sandpiper walking along for ten minutes and never once does it bob or pump its rear end, then it almost certainly isn't a Spotted Sandpiper, unlike this bird, which is. Negative knowledge will come with experience, but only if you start to observe. *Jalisco, Mexico, 11 January 2016.*

In winter, Varied Thrushes (here a male) favor shady leaf litter where their complex plumage patterns afford surprisingly good camouflage. They tend not to associate with American Robins, which often forage in more open situations. *Marin County, California, 2 February 2007.*

its head down and tail held high, it's a Stilt Sandpiper. If it's running around on the mud snapping at flies, often with its rear end in the air, or swimming and picking at the water's surface, it's a Wilson's Phalarope. Yes, Stilt Sandpipers and Lesser Yellowlegs can swim on occasion, but not usually for very long or as part of their regular feeding behavior.

It's called the power of observation because it's *powerful*. And not just for birding, but for life in general—as Yogi Berra famously said: "You can observe a lot by just watching."

BIRDS FINDING BIRDS FOR YOU

Not only can behavior help you ID a bird, it can also help you *find* birds. By watching what birds do, you may start to key in on behaviors that lead you to other birds. For example, you're driving along the highway and a ways ahead you see a crow swooping down, back and forth over the top of a tree. There's a good chance that a Red-tailed Hawk, or something less common in your area, is the object of the crow's attention, so you could slow down or stop and take a look.

Or you're helping with a waterbird survey, counting lots of ducks, shorebirds, and gulls, when almost everything takes off and flies around. It's very frustrating if you're counting, but while you wait for things to settle you should look for an eagle overhead, or perhaps a large falcon. In your own area, you'll soon learn the difference between a typical "falcon flush" and an "eagle flush," with the latter usually involving gulls as well as shorebirds and dabbling ducks, and over a wider area than the former.

TRUE OR FALSE?

The more time you spend in the field, the more you'll start to learn subconsciously about behavior, simply by watching. As a starter, which of the following statements is generally true and which is generally false? You may not have seen all of these species or groups of birds, but the nature of the statements may help you think about how to observe. You may also realize that you don't know some common birds as well as you might have thought.

1. Cormorants sleep when swimming.
2. Varied Thrushes often feed with flocks of American Robins.
3. Crows soar.
4. Mallards dive.
5. Eastern Bluebirds hover.
6. Woodpeckers forage on the ground.
7. Canada Geese glide while flying high.
8. European Starlings hop.

You're watching a Snowy Plover when suddenly it freezes, crouches a little, and turns its head slowly sideways to look up. You should look up as well: there's a good chance a Peregrine Falcon or some other predator is flying over. It might be a long way overhead or off in the distance, but a Snowy Plover's life depends upon spotting predators, and the birds that have survived are good at it. *Marin County, California, 28 February 2010.*

Here are the answers, at least as we understand them in the areas we know. Cormorants: false, they typically sleep out of the water. Varied Thrushes: false, but they may associate with flights of robins. Crows: false, but ravens soar regularly. Mallards: true, but see below. Eastern Bluebirds: true, as do all bluebirds, especially in open country when windy. Woodpeckers: false—except for flickers, which often feed on the ground. Canada Geese: false, but cormorants often glide. European Starlings: false, they typically walk. How did you do?

Behavior can vary with season or by region, or even by age and sex. For example, in the breeding season, males of many usually skulking species often perch up conspicuously whereas females more often remain in cover. Have you seen Mallards dive? The ducklings can dive frequently when feeding, and even adult Mallards are able to dive easily when a Peregrine Falcon stoops on them!

Despite the importance of behavior to ID, so many beginning bird talks we see start with "Look at the bill" or "Learn the bird's anatomy, these are the scapulars . . . ," and so on. This is valuable stuff, but the first eight of our twelve steps don't involve that level of detail. You can ID many if not most of the birds you see before worrying about the details. And one aspect of bird behavior is so important that we single it out for its own step, coming next.

Listen—What Do You Hear? (Sound)

A s humans, our primary sensory input is visual, at least during daytime, and we are ostensibly diurnal animals. Sounds? Not so much. Our first impressions are usually visual—a beautiful vista with a shimmering lake, she has amazing eyes, it's dark and I can't see a bloody thing, and so on. We also have perfectly functional ears, however, and sooner or later most birders realize that sound, Step 8, can be a key feature in finding and identifying birds.

Sound is amazing. You can hear in the dark, you can hear through vegetation, you can hear clearly with the sun in your eyes, you can hear from all directions—not just from the direction your eyes and ears are pointing. Sound can also carry over considerable distance, enabling ID well beyond the range that traditional physical field marks are visible.

For example, experienced birders might turn around, look up, and say "Waxwings" as they point at a flock of distant specks flying away. Did they see the birds' crests and black throats? The waxy tips to some

---

OPPOSITE: Although not shy, the taxonomically enigmatic Wrentit is generally a retiring and visually inconspicuous bird that most people overlook. But if you know its songs and, perhaps more importantly, its quiet, ratchetlike churring calls, you will discover that Wrentits are quite common—at least in the right habitat and in the right geographic range. *Marin County, California, 14 December 2014.*

---

wing feathers? The yellow tail tips? No; a thin, high-pitched call carried through the air is all that was needed to ID waxwings in flight. It takes a bit of practice, but it's well worth the investment.

SONGS VERSUS CALLS

One common question about bird sounds is: What's the difference between a *song* and a *call*? Well, it's subjective, and different people even have different ideas about what a song is versus a *song phrase* and other components of songs. Like almost any subject, it can get complicated, with lots of technical terms, but you don't need to worry about all that.

In general, songs are longer and more complex, are often repeated more persistently, and are related to attracting a mate or defending a territory. Calls are typically shorter and serve a variety of other functions, such as warning of predators (alarm calls) or keeping members of a flock

---

Different groups of birds make different sounds, such as the songs of warblers compared to those of flycatchers. This can also apply to different genera within families. The Eared Quetzal (genus *Euptilotis*, shown here) sounds very different from an Elegant Trogon, and from any other species in the genus *Trogon. Chihuahua, Mexico, 21 August 2013.*

together (contact calls or flight calls). These are simplified definitions for convenience, and there are exceptions. For woodpeckers, their acoustic drumming is equivalent to a song.

If you study any songbird closely, you'll learn it has many different calls, with many different functions—it's a language, akin to human language. While birds probably don't sit around and debate philosophy, they can surely communicate a lot more information than we might think. Ever go birding with a field biologist who has studied the breeding biology of species X? She or he may not be a birder as we think of it, but they can pick out a whole suite of sounds made by their study species, sounds you had perhaps never thought about, or the source of which you didn't know.

As a rule, one big difference between songs and calls is seasonality: calls are given year-round, whereas songs, because they are used to defend territories and find mates, are given mainly in the breeding season. Many spring migrants (such as warblers) are pumped up with hormones and will sing during spring migration, or even start singing before they leave the wintering grounds. But warblers on fall migration very rarely, if ever, sing.

There are exceptions to the seasonality rule, of course, and by paying attention you may start to discern seasonal patterns to these exceptions. Many songbirds learn their songs by hearing them, and some species have a second period of song in late summer, which corresponds to when young have hatched and are being exposed to the songs they will learn. Late summer and fall are also when we often hear "messy" and atypical songs, as young birds are practicing. The practice period, as songs crystalize, can extend into the first spring. This is a contributing factor to the confusing complexity of spring warbler songs.

For several resident species, a usually brief period of adult song follows completion of their molt (molting is typically a quiet period for many songbirds), perhaps simply a sign for the neighbors that says, "I'm still here, and I plan on keeping my territory."

Many birds defend nonbreeding territories, and migrants arriving on their wintering ground often sing for a while to establish a territory. This is common among flycatchers and warblers that winter south of the United States, but it also occurs in North America. For example, where we live, some migrant Black Phoebes and Fox Sparrows sing persistently for a few weeks in fall, indicating that these are individuals likely to winter locally rather than head on farther south.

DIFFERENT TYPES OF SONGBIRDS

The terms *oscine* and *suboscine* are often used when talking of songbirds, or passerines. The suboscines are more primitive songbirds, with a relatively simple voice apparatus. Along with most nonpasserines, suboscines generally do not produce sounds that humans would describe as overly musical or complex. New World flycatchers are suboscines, as are

Some taxonomic authorities split the Mangrove Warbler (here, an adult male) from the "regular" Yellow Warbler. The songs of both are rather variable and can sound similar to one another, but the "fixed" call notes of both are quite distinctive and easier to learn. *Jalisco, Mexico, 7 February 2016.*

A big, yellow-bellied flycatcher perched on wires is likely to be a kingbird, in this case a Tropical or Couch's Kingbird. The tapered shape of the outer primaries, visible on the underside of the far wingtip, indicates an adult male. In combination with a weakly forked tail and relatively short bill, this strongly suggests Couch's Kingbird, but few if any birders would bet their house on that ID. The surest approach is to wait for it to call—it did, and it was a Couch's. *Cameron County, Texas, 18 February 2009.*

several families found outside of North America, such as the antbirds of the Neotropics. In these species, songs are considered to be genetically hardwired rather than learned.

Oscines, on the other hand, have a more complex voice apparatus. Their songs are typically learned rather than hardwired, and often are quite complex or sound more pleasing to human ears. Oscine songbirds, sometimes called the true songbirds, include wrens, thrushes, and warblers. Because oscine songs are learned, it is possible for one species to learn the song of another. This can be confusing in the field, although it is relatively rare. More frequent, and also potentially confusing, is the existence of distinct regional song dialects within some species, just like human dialects—most people would consider that American English sounds different between Maine and Mississippi, but that only a single species of human is involved.

Unlike their songs, however, the call notes of many oscines are believed to be hardwired and thus are not as variable as the songs might be. Think of the basic *chek* or *chek-chek* calls of a Northern Mockingbird compared to its remarkably varied song.

SOUND ADVICE

Listening is a lot like looking: it's best to start simple and work your way in slowly. At first, when you start to listen, a dawn chorus can seem like one blended wall of sound. With so much going on, how can you pick

Spotted Towhee is an excellent example of a species that exhibits considerable individual and regional variation in its song. Local dialects in California, even within a single county, can be confusing to experienced birders, not just to somebody starting out. Of course, some of the variation (including of call notes) may hint that more than one species is involved. *Marin County, California, 19 March 2008.*

out different sounds or tell one species from another? The call note of this or that warbler is just another *chip* in the wall.

In the same way that you may see only part of a bird and perhaps be misled, you may also hear only part of a song or call. The bird might be turning its head, or it may simply be too far away for you to hear its sounds clearly. Just as some birders are trigger-happy with visual ID, so others are with sounds. A good rule is if you think you hear something unusual, stop and listen, and make sure you hear it clearly two or three times, not just once.

When learning sounds, it's helpful to start with a common species in your neighborhood. It also may be easier not to start in the early morning or in spring, when there is more sound than at other times, making it harder to filter out distractions. Begin with something you are looking at, which helps link the sound to the bird (and ensures correct identification), not with distant sounds of unseen birds. As you build a bigger frame of reference, it becomes easier to add sounds to your mental library, and before long you can become familiar with the common birds in your neighborhood.

Writing down a description of the song or call *while hearing it* can be very helpful in learning. There are different ways to do this. David Sibley's book *Sibley's Birding Basics*[1] contains lots of good information, including a helpful chapter with tips on how to describe sounds. Simple songs or calls, such as a Mourning Dove song, can be written in "words," as in *h'hooo hooo-ooo-ooo,* which could be annotated by adding "an unhurried mournful cooing that slows or fades slightly toward the end."

Songs of greater complexity can be described with various adjectives. If you're learning songs and calls for yourself, then it doesn't matter if your descriptions don't work for other people—they only need to work for you. If you want to communicate them meaningfully to others, however, then a more standardized terminology is desirable, akin to the terms used to describe parts of a bird. (If your "head" is

A chunky, medium-size, rather drab flycatcher (or moth-catcher in this case) with a peaked nape, long wings accentuating a relatively short tail, and a mottled dark vest all add up to an Olive-sided Flycatcher, but which one? Without hearing it sing (see the sonograms opposite), there's not much you can do other than make an assumption based on range: we assume this is a "Cooper's Pewee." *Los Angeles County, California, 26 April 2004.*

somebody else's "rump" then . . . well, you get the idea.) Standard sound terms have been proposed,[2] but this approach has yet to be widely adopted by birders.

Comparisons with known species can also be helpful. For example, "a hurried, bubbling warble" might work for western Purple Finch, whereas "a slightly scratchy and jumbled warble, often more prolonged and wheezy than Purple Finch" might work for House Finch.

Some people like to "draw" sounds with symbols, in effect making their own sonograms. If you become really keen on "birding by ear," as it is often known, then you can record birds yourself or make sonograms from recordings available online. A good place to start is with the software Raven Lite.[3]

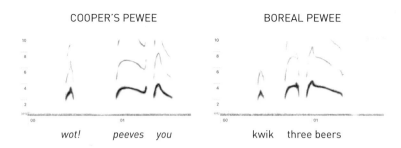

COOPER'S PEWEE			BOREAL PEWEE	
wot!	*peeves*	*you*	kwik	three beers

Sometimes it's easy to hear that two sounds are different, but not so easy to describe the difference. Sonograms (literally, sound graphs) allow you to actually see and even measure differences, which can really help with learning and with describing what you hear. The vertical axis represents frequency (in kilohertz), the horizontal axis time (in seconds). Here we compare the two song types of Olive-sided Flycatcher (in the genus *Contopus,* and really just a pewee; remember Step 1), which do not correspond to recognized subspecies, but which may represent cryptic species.

West Coast and western mountain birds ("Cooper's Pewee") have a more emphatic first note, a longer pause before a longer and mostly overslurred (versus mostly upslurred) second note, and a shorter last note (Macaulay Library 205441; Sierra County, California, 9 June 2000). Boreal forest populations ("Boreal Pewee") have a more evenly measured song *(Macaulay Library 59777; Ontario, Canada, 7 June 1953).*

These days, numerous bird sound apps are available, as well as websites where you can access vast libraries of reference sounds, such as the Macaulay Library at the Cornell Lab of Ornithology[4] and the worldwide database of Xeno-canto.[5] One thing you may quickly learn with apps is how good your ears actually are, not to mention getting an appreciation for how variable and amazing bird songs can be, even within a species or population. That is, you can be watching a bird sing in the field and then listen to three examples of that species' song, only to find that no two sound the same, and none sounds like your bird! In the same way that a picture in a book never looks quite like the bird, the song may never

Dowitchers in North America comprise two very similar-looking species of medium-size sandpipers, best separated by call. Early field guides even recommended throwing a stone so the birds would fly and call, allowing you to ID them! With attention to visible details, however, the Short-billed Dowitcher (right) can be distinguished from the two Long-billed Dowitchers (left) without having to disturb them. *Marin County, California, 16 September 2015.*

match what you're hearing, especially if it's an oscine such as a warbler or sparrow.

USING SOUND IN THE FIELD

One obvious way that sound helps in the field is with identifying species that look very similar but sound quite different. Examples include several flycatchers and thrushes, some of which may be safely identified in the field only by voice. Although sound is an integral part of the world of birds and birding, some birders don't count on their list any birds they hear but don't see. Yet they happily count birds they see but don't hear, even if sound is the primary or perhaps only means of realistically identifying those species in the field.[6]

Being aware of sounds can also help you find birds, and not just skulking species that are hard to see. For example, scanning through a feeding flock of swallows over a pond, you may see lots of Tree and Barn Swallows, and a few Cliff Swallows. But then you hear the distinctive buzzy call of a Northern Rough-winged Swallow—it's in there somewhere, but it might take quite a while to visually locate it in the swirling mass.

Alarm calls are good things to key in on. Upset chickadees might be mobbing a roosting owl, or the alarm calls of Barn Swallows could clue you in to the presence of a raptor overhead, such as a Peregrine Falcon. Many shorebirds are very vocal, but some are not. If you think you're watching a Stilt Sandpiper or a Wilson's Phalarope, and it flies off calling

Warblers are popular birds in North America, at least to look at. Their songs, on the other hand, like those of several other oscines, can be very variable and confusing. Connecticut Warbler has a relatively loud and distinctive song, and will often sit and sing with no apparent heed to the people watching it. This singing behavior is very different from its behavior during migration, when the species is notoriously skulking and hard to find. *St. Louis County, Minnesota, 6 June 2016.*

The onomatopoeic names Poorwill, Whip-poor-will, and Chuck-will's-Widow bear testament to the importance of voice for many nightjars, whose dead-leaf plumage patterns render them notoriously cryptic during the daytime. Visual field marks are not overly important for this Pauraque, but come sundown its loud song readily identifies it to species. *Hidalgo County, Texas, 9 November 2010.*

loudly, then it probably was neither of those species, both of which rarely utter more than quiet grunts when flushed.

Flight calls, especially as given at night, are an aspect of bird sound that is gaining in popularity among both birders and scientists. Particularly during migration periods, it's possible to go out at night and hear birds flying overhead, sometimes only a few per hour, sometimes thousands per hour; numbers of calls vary with location (the phenomenon is much more prevalent in the East than the West), weather, and other factors. Some species are very vocal in flight, such as thrushes, whereas others are ostensibly silent, such as vireos. It's a whole other world of birds that can be appreciated through knowing the calls they make.[7]

Sound, like so much of birding, is a matter of experience, but being aware of bird sounds at any level, and paying attention to them, makes birding more productive, and more fun. Part of the fun with sounds is discovering a whole new meaning to the idea of "similar species." For example, not many people would consider Wrentit and Western Gull to be (visually) similar, but they can certainly be confused when heard at a distance.

Let's recap the steps we've looked at so far—the ingredients that combine to help you ID a bird. The first four are very basic: start with a bird, your location, the habitat, and date. Always consider two external factors, lighting and distance, over which you have no control. And then throw in behavior, including sound.

Each step on its own is pretty simple, but together these steps are quite powerful. You'll notice that the first eight of the twelve steps do not involve the classic "Look at the bill shape and plumage pattern" approach, and do not require you to learn all sorts of technical terms for plumage or anatomy.

These basic first eight steps are things that pretty much anyone knows, or can appreciate with just a bit of observation. You can do a lot with them, but now we've reached the stage of looking at details, which can be viewed as dressings on the basic ID package.

STEP 9

Shaping Your Experience (Structure)

Now we're finally getting to the point where many people start learning, or teaching, bird ID. But you've reached this point through a number of assumptions and a bunch of information that you may not have realized was important. As we've pointed out, many birds can be identified by a combination of basic facts, the power of observation, and an awareness of the environment.

Sometimes, though, you can have a good view of a bird, know the location, habitat, season, behavior, and so on, but you're still not sure what you're looking at. In such cases, attention to details such as shape, size, and plumage can help resolve the ID. Step 9 is structure, which we take here to include an integrated combination of a bird's size and shape.

The introduction to any bird field guide includes a section, usually with one or more images, covering bird anatomy—the terms you use to describe a bird. To communicate clearly with others, it's useful to learn at least the basic terms (*primaries, scapulars, tertials,* etc.), but be aware that some parts of a bird are called different things by different people.

OPPOSITE: Black-necked Stilts have very long legs, but all structural characters are relative, as can be appreciated here when a stilt is compared to these American Flamingoes. *Yucatan, Mexico, 26 November 2010.*

For example, some people use *eyebrow* and others use *supercilium* for the same feature; the former term is easier and more intuitive, the latter more old school and, some might say, supercilious. We're not going to get into terminology here (it's covered in your field guides and you can read it there), but instead we'll look at related topics not covered so well, if at all, in field guides.

SIZE MATTERS—BUT WHAT IS SIZE?

How much bigger is a European Starling than a Song Sparrow? Well, the field guides say a starling is around 9 inches, the sparrow around 6 inches. Given this, you might think a starling is 1.5 times as big as a sparrow. But do you know how those field guide measurements are derived?

The conventional field guide "size" is a measure of "total length," taken from museum skins laid on their back and measured bill tip to tail tip, with no undue stretching force applied. It doesn't take into account leg length, or reflect how tall a bird stands, or whether it has long wings projecting past the tail tip. This standard measure is a carryover from old manuals designed for ornithologists who collected birds and had them in hand, freshly dead. It has continued into modern field guides for the simple reason that nobody has come up with a better way to convey the size of a bird. But how often do you see birds in the field lying on their back to allow comparison?

Unlike in humans and most other mammals, juvenile birds (once they have left the nest or achieved independence) are basically the same size as adults. In some species, such as curlews and large gulls, it may take much of the first year for bill length or bill depth to fill out to adult size, but overall body size is basically the same as an adult. In some species of large hawks, juveniles can be wider-winged than adults and actually appear larger in the field, as is the case with juvenile Bald Eagles.

Most birds show some sex-related size differences. As a rule, males

These specimens represent the way your field guide lengths, or "sizes," are derived. Is this European Starling (below) 1.5 times the size of the Song Sparrow (above)? Most people, we suspect, would say it looks at least twice as big—yet it measures 9 inches compared to 6 inches for a Song Sparrow. Remember, though, that a bird's surface area (which is what we tend to evaluate in the field as "size") is quite different from its length.

average larger, but in some groups the females average larger. In some cases, sex-related size differences can be detected in the field (such as with accipiters, or bill length in several sandpipers), but for most birds they are average and not really noticeable.

Virtually all field guides, however, give just a single length for any species, yet every species varies, from a little to a lot, something we cover more fully in Step 11. For example, our own measurements of series of museum specimens give a length for Song Sparrow (not including the huge Alaskan birds) of 5.7 to 6.3 inches, and for a European Starling of 8 to 9 inches. That's an inherent size variation of more than 10 percent.

For bigger birds this variation can be appreciably greater, and the whole size issue is compounded by different people measuring things

Behavior can be very helpful to identify various shorebird species, but mainly when they are foraging. With a resting group (or a photo), relative size, shape, and things such as bill proportions are often more helpful than plumage.

Long-billed Curlew (left) can have relatively distinct crown stripes, and this bird also looks rather cold-toned compared to the Marbled Godwit (right). Both of these features could suggest a Whimbrel, but even allowing for the possibility of photographic size illusion, a Whimbrel should not appear this much larger than a godwit (see Table 1, p. 83). *Marin County, California, 29 August 2015.*

differently. For example, for Long-billed Curlew versus Whimbrel and Marbled Godwit, Table 1 shows the lengths given by five bird ID guides.

Thus, depending on which book you read, a curlew is about 6 inches longer than a Whimbrel (17 inches versus 23), but it may be only 1 inch longer (17 inches versus 18) or as much as 9 inches longer (14 inches versus 23), largely relating to a bird's sex (females have longer bills) and age (first-year birds have shorter bills).

And remember, the surface area of a bird is closer to what your mind evaluates in the field as "size," which would be a square of length

TABLE 1. Comparison of lengths (in inches) given in field guides for Long-billed Curlew, Whimbrel, and Marbled Godwit.

	Peterson[1]	Sibley[2]	Kaufman[3]	National Geographic[4]	Howell and Webb[5]
Curlew	22–24	23	23	23	18–23
Whimbrel	17–18	17.5	17	17.5	14–17
Godwit	17.5–18.5	18	18	18	15–18

(assuming the bird is square). When you throw things like wingspan and wing area into the mix, then measurements in field guides can be even more difficult to interpret. Plus, birds are three-dimensional, so what you see in the field could be the cube of field guide length, potentially creating an even greater discrepancy between "size" in the field and "length" in the book. This all supposes the birds you are comparing have the same proportions; if not, then "size" comparisons are even more difficult to judge based simply on lengths given in a field guide.

Then again, as we said, nobody has come up with anything better. While field guide lengths may not reflect "size" as you see it in the field, they offer at least a rough measure of relative size, assuming birds are of similar proportion. From the foregoing, however, it should be clear that measurements in a field guide should be interpreted with caution.

CRITICAL MASS

Some field guides also give values for mass (or weight, to us non-physicists), which can be a useful measure to supplement length and wingspan, assuming birds share a similar structure. A bird's mass, however, can vary hugely depending on whether it has eaten recently, is fattened for breeding, is a lean immature after migration, and so on. And usually only a single value is given, not a realistic or meaningful range.

Moreover, because of structural differences that can reflect things such as habitat or life-history characteristics, heavier birds do not necessarily appear bigger than lighter birds.

For example, Sooty Shearwater and Buller's Shearwater are about the same size in a field guide (length around 18 inches and wingspan around 40 inches), but one has an average weight of about 800 grams (range 670 to 980 grams), while the other has an average weight of around 425 grams (range 340 to 500 grams). This might lead you to think one is twice as massive as the other, but which one (if either) looks bigger in the field?

Despite having similar lengths and wingspans, Buller's Shearwater (right) has broad wings, and Sooty Shearwater (left) has narrow wings, which can make Buller's look bigger. However, Buller's is lightly built, adapted to live in calmer subtropical latitudes where its broad wings help it fly with buoyant ease. Conversely, Sooty is a heavy-bodied bird (often weighing twice as much as Buller's) adapted to windy high latitudes where its narrow wings enable it to arc steeply and strongly. *Marin County, California, 7 September 2007 (left) and 20 October 2013 (right).*

This composite of Chimney Swifts (all images taken within 45 minutes) shows how wing shape can change dramatically depending on things like bird behavior (such as stalling versus direct flight) and angle of view. *Traill County, North Dakota, 9 June 2016.*

ABSOLUTE OR RELATIVE?

Bearing in mind the caveats above, accurately judging the approximate size of a bird can be very useful in ID. Most people would consider Turkey Vultures to be large birds, hummingbirds and sparrows to be small birds. Distance can sometimes fool you when judging size, but most of the time you can make a reasonable guesstimate of a bird's size, as in "It was about the size of a crow," or "It was slightly smaller than a robin, but bigger than a sparrow." This relative size evaluation (especially if made by direct comparison with known species) is a lot more realistic than saying "I saw a bird, it was about 8.5 inches long . . ." Come on, was it laid out flat on its back next to a ruler?

Relative sizes, often in combination with proportions, are very useful for many challenging IDs, such as among gulls, shorebirds, flycatchers, and sparrows.

FIXED OR CHANGEABLE?

Some things, like the shape of a bird's beak, are pretty fixed. Other things, like the wing shape of a flying bird, can change depending on whether a bird is soaring, gliding, flying into the wind, flying across the wind, and so on. Birds like Red-tailed Hawk and Turkey Vulture, and even crows, are good subjects to watch and see how their wing shape changes depending on flight manner, angle of view, and wind conditions. Watching a bird over time helps even out such differences, which can be exaggerated by a series of still images.

"I saw a small bird hop up in a bush the other day; it was mid-December in central California, in a brushy hedgerow. The bird was brown above with rusty on the wings and tail and dark spots below; it had a bit of an eye-ring; the tail was a bit cocked, the legs were pinkish, the bill was pinkish or orangey at the base . . ." So what shape was the bill? Stout and conical like a Fox Sparrow's (left), or slender like a Hermit Thrush's (right)? *Marin County, California, 14 December 2014 (left) and 5 October 2012 (right).*

When you get down to a close view and wonder what you're seeing, look at structure. The left-hand bird is a small songbird, drab greenish overall, paler below, with pale wing bars, a pale eye-ring, and dark legs. But that description could apply equally to the right-hand bird.

While rather similar in size and coloration, the left-hand bird is a bit crested; slimmer and longer-tailed overall; and has a more pointed bill (which shows orange below at this angle), thinner legs, and weaker feet. It is also perching more upright, but this could simply be an artifact of the photo. Alternatively, we could say the right-hand bird is a bit chunkier and bigger-headed, and has a rounded head, a blunter bill, thicker (and more bluish-gray) legs, and stronger feet.

It's helpful to combine as many of the steps as possible: behavior and voice also differ appreciably between the (presumed) Pacific-slope Flycatcher (left) and the Hutton's Vireo (right), which occur alongside one another in the same habitats. *Monterey County, California, 24 May 2014 (left); Marin County, California, 10 July 2007 (right).*

A SENSE OF PROPORTION

While relative overall size is useful, a sense of proportional or structural differences is often the key to solving some tricky ID issues, as among various species of flycatchers. Species that appear similar in their general

blunt wingtip with broad longest primary

tapered wingtip with narrow longest primary

Not so many years ago, separating Ruby-throated from Black-chinned Hummingbirds in female and immature plumage was considered impossible in the field—and it's still not easy. But, from examination of museum specimens, the ornithologist Allan R. Phillips noticed a subtle difference in the shape of the primaries, as can be seen on these adult females in fall. Black-chinned (left) has broader and blunter-tipped feathers that curve slightly to form a broad, "clubbed" wingtip. Ruby-throated (right) has slightly narrower and less rounded feathers that form a tapered wingtip.

On perched birds, and especially with digital images, such differences can be appreciated and species ID confirmed, at least if the wingtips are not heavily worn or in molt. *Santa Cruz County, Arizona, 22 August 2014 (left); Marin County, California, 9 August 2010 (right).*

coloration or size usually differ in proportions, such as relative bill size and shape, tail length, leg length, or wing shape. Sometimes the differences are fairly obvious, as between a sparrow bill and a thrush bill. In other cases, seeing this sort of thing can take a bit of practice, as with how far the tail projects past the tips of the undertail coverts on a Pine Warbler versus a Bay-breasted Warbler, or the shape and relative width of primary feathers on hummingbirds. But like so much of bird ID, that's all it is—practice, combined with observation.

Structure should always be combined with location, habitat, and season, plus behavior, voice, and anything else. It's important to use as many of the twelve steps as possible, including the next step, which tends to be something we see right away when looking at a bird—its plumage.

Feathers Make a Bird (Plumage)

A t its simplest, a bird is defined as an animal with feathers. When we look at a bird, what we mostly see is its plumage—the coat of feathers it is wearing to produce its shape and color. Feathers are remarkable structures, very light but at the same time very strong, protecting a bird from the elements and enabling it to fly. But feathers don't last forever. They wear out, and sooner or later need to be replaced by a process known as molt.

As with taxonomy, some people start to run or leave the room when that dreaded four-letter word, *molt*, is uttered. Like most things, though, fear of molt is simply fear of the unknown, an unfounded fear we hope to kill right here. Step 10, then, discusses some things relating to plumage (including molt) that can help you develop a more solid understanding of bird ID.

Don't worry, we're not going to get into any technical molt stuff such as prebasic molts, or alternate and formative plumages—you can look

OPPOSITE: Despite the popular idea of "confusing fall warblers," most warbler species look more or less the same year-round—think American Redstart, Hooded Warbler, and Townsend's Warbler. Only a handful, including Bay-breasted Warbler (here, an adult male in breeding plumage), molt in fall into a drab nonbreeding plumage. *Lake County, Minnesota, 7 June 2016.*

elsewhere for that information.[1] In fact, for birders it makes more sense to use terms such as *breeding plumage, juvenile plumage, male plumage,* and so on. (In our experience, most birders who use terms such as *basic* and *alternate plumage* in the field are misusing them much of the time.) Just like taxonomy and many other subjects, there are different concepts— none right or wrong, just different.

WHAT'S THAT RED BIRD?

No matter how much we may be taught about the importance to bird ID of things such as size, structure, habitat, and behavior, there's no denying that color and plumage patterns are some of the first things we notice when we see a bird. And indeed, color patterns are often very useful for ID. They are highlighted by field guides and shown in field guide illustrations, so we won't talk much about them here. Instead, we'll offer some background information related to plumage and feathers—things that are not usually covered by field guides.

WHAT IS MOLT, AND WHY?

Molt is feather growth. It's that simple. Feathers grow from follicles in the skin, much like human hair, but they are renewed periodically by molts, rather than growing continually like hair. Molt is also a huge and fascinating subject, but for now here's the five-minute version.

As a rule, all species of birds molt their whole plumage once a year by an orderly process, be they penguins or hummingbirds, owls or warblers. This single annual molt is the underlying strategy on which all other patterns of molting are built. Many species get by with only this one complete molt per year. Other species, however, fit a second molt into their annual cycle, and a few species have a third molt; these additional molts usually don't involve all of the plumage, just feathers on the head and body, not the big feathers of the wings and tail.

The reason birds molt is that their feathers wear out and can no longer keep them warm or enable them to fly. A combination of fading by

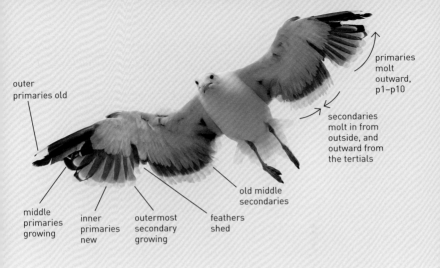

outer
primaries old

primaries
molt
outward,
p1–p10

secondaries
molt in from
outside, and
outward from
the tertials

old middle
secondaries

middle
primaries
growing

inner
primaries
new

outermost
secondary
growing

feathers
shed

ABOVE: This adult Western Gull illustrates the sequence of wing molt common to many species of North American birds, from hawks and gulls to woodpeckers and songbirds. Molt starts at the innermost primary (p1) and proceeds outward sequentially to the outermost primary (p10). At about the time that p6–p7 are shed, molt starts at the outermost secondary (s1) and moves inward, toward the body; molt also starts with the innermost secondaries (the tertials) and moves outward, to meet in the middle. *Monterey County, California, 29 September 2006.*

sunlight and abrasion through contact with vegetation, blowing sand, and other environmental factors causes feathers to deteriorate. It's just like clothes that fade and start to wear out with use.

Simply thinking about a bird's life history can help you develop ideas about its molt. All else being equal, it follows that birds living in relatively protected environments, such as shady forests, won't need to molt as much as birds living in exposed sunny environments, such as marshes and grasslands. Birds that migrate long distances and experience sun year-round are more likely to have two molts a year than are residents or nocturnal birds, which shun the sun.

OPPOSITE: Feather wear and fading can have an appreciable influence on the appearance of birds that you might think look pretty much the same year-round. Here are some Savannah Sparrows in Marin County, California. Juveniles have soft and weakly patterned plumage, but by fall (following molt) they and adults all look similar, in fresh, boldly marked plumage. By winter, buffy tones fade slightly and black back streaks become wider through the wearing away of pale feather edgings. By spring, the plumage has worn and faded even more, with buffy tones mostly lost. By midsummer, birds are at their most faded, and wearing away of feathers around the base of the bill can even make the bill appear larger than usual. A complete molt in late summer renews the plumage (producing the fresh fall aspect again), and some birds shed all of their tail feathers at the same time during this molt.

Given these simple facts, you could deduce that woodpeckers and owls are likely to have only one molt a year, but that ducks and migrant shorebirds are likely to have two (or more) molts. See? It's easy.

WHEN DO BIRDS MOLT?

Molt is all about time and food. When and where molt occurs depends on how much time is needed to grow feathers, and where food can be reliably found to safely fuel a molt. Related to time is the size of a bird. While small feathers on the head and body can be grown fairly quickly, the molt of big wing and tail feathers can take a long time; these feathers can grow only so fast, at around 2 to 5 mm per day for smaller birds, 4 to 10 mm per day for larger birds. As a rule, then, bigger birds take longer to molt than do small birds.

When we talk about molt and field ID, it's usually wing molt we are referring to, especially molt of the primaries. Most bird species have ten primaries, which are the long feathers attached to the hand bones and which form the shape of the wingtip. The primaries typically molt once a year, from innermost to outermost, from the bend of the wing out to the tip. It's useful here to know that young birds of most species keep their juvenile wings and tail for their first year of life, so they won't necessarily

juvenile, summer

fall

winter

spring

midsummer

late summer

be undergoing wing molt in their first fall or winter, when the adults are molting. Thus, presence of wing molt can be very useful, but absence of wing molt is not necessarily helpful for species ID (though it can help with determining a bird's age).

Just like learning the characteristics of families and genera, learning a few patterns is easier than learning the details of molt for every single species. Here are three general rules.

new inner primaries

faded old outer primaries

molt in middle primaries

Photographed in late May off North Carolina, this Band-rumped Storm-Petrel shows obvious wing molt, which has reached the middle primaries. On this date, the wing molt is too advanced for the very similar-looking Leach's Storm-Petrel (even an immature, which could just be starting to molt on this date). Thus, molt helps identify this as an adult Band-rumped from a winter-breeding population.

1. Most birds molt toward the end of their breeding season or after it. Late summer is often when food is most plentiful, allowing adults to molt and young birds to fend for themselves. For species that don't breed in their first year, the nonbreeding immature birds tend to molt earlier than adults engaged in breeding. You can see this easily with Herring Gulls and Red-tailed Hawks, in which immatures and nonbreeders undergo wing molt from spring through fall, whereas breeding adults molt a bit later, from summer into early winter. An age-related difference in molt timing is common in seabirds, with year-old birds usually molting a few months earlier than breeding adults; this can help with age-related as well as species-related ID, as for cryptic species of storm-petrels.

2. Resident species and short-distance migrants typically molt their wings right after breeding, on or near the breeding grounds, and before the onset of winter, mainly June through October in North America. Think jays, chickadees, cardinals, most sparrows. Many migrants do this as well, if there is sufficient time and food.

3. Some long-distance migrants, on the other hand, molt their wings on the nonbreeding grounds, such as in South America, which is warm in the northern winter, with lots of food. Therefore, you don't see them molting their wings in North America. Think some shorebirds, swallows, and flycatchers. In some cases, wing molt can be interrupted—started in summer, suspended for migration, and completed in winter; terns are a good example of this.

So if you know that Lesser Nighthawk is a short-distance migrant, but Common Nighthawk is a long-distance migrant, you can deduce that a nighthawk you see undergoing wing molt in late summer will be a Lesser. You don't have to see the white wing band, hear it call, try to evaluate wingtip shape—molt identifies it easily.

BIRDS THAT CHEAT

We often read that molt is costly, requiring a lot of energy to grow feathers. This may not be true simply for the direct cost of growing feathers, but some indirect costs of molt, such as heat loss or impaired flight, may be quite significant. Perhaps for such reasons, a number of species change their appearance seasonally not by molt but through the wearing away of feather tips that have veiled different underlying colors or patterns.

Some of the most striking examples in North America are male Snow Bunting and male Lapland Longspur, but more familiar examples include European Starling and House Sparrow. It seems likely that the feather tips are genetically programmed to wear off after a certain number of months, revealing an undercoat of bolder patterns or brighter

molt in inner primaries

full-winged, no molt

ABOVE: Photographed in Arizona in August, the left-hand nighthawk is undergoing obvious wing molt, which makes it a Lesser Nighthawk. Lack of wing molt, however, is not always helpful for species ID, because young Lesser Nighthawks do not molt their wings until about a year of age; thus, they will be full-winged in fall, like all ages of Common Nighthawk.

BELOW: The striking change in appearance between a winter male Lapland Longspur (left) and a breeding male (right) involves little if any molt, and is brought about by wearing away of buffy and whitish feather tips that in fresh plumage veil the boldly patterned breeding plumage. *Marin County, California, 20 December 2013 (left); Barrow, Alaska, 20 June 2014 (right).*

colors. This is presumably less costly than undergoing two molts, but it serves the same function in changing a bird's appearance. These species thus get two for the price of one.

MOLT AND PLUMAGE COLOR—THE DISCONNECT

Here's something a lot of experienced birders don't understand: color and molt operate on independent pathways. Usually they are linked, but not always. Basically, molt occurs during period X, and pigment deposition on feathers occurs during period Y. When X and Y coincide you get the right colors from a molt. When they don't, you can get the wrong colors. This disconnect may help to reveal birds that are sick or otherwise not quite right, and perhaps pull them out of the breeding population.

Just like people, different immature birds develop at different rates relating to hormone levels. The change from juvenile plumage color and pattern to adult color and pattern may occur over a period of months, even years, and the timing of a bird's molt can have an effect on the color of the plumage it grows. This realization can help us understand why the

An example of how colors and molts can operate independently. This diagram represents the complete annual molt of a male Red Crossbill. The molt window usually corresponds with the red pigment window, but if it doesn't an adult male crossbill molting before or after this period can be golden yellow or patchy red and yellow. A birder might be tempted to call any such bird an immature, but it could just as easily be an adult. The switch in pigment is so quick that a feather can be one color at its base, another at its tip. Reproduced from Steve N. G. Howell, *Peterson Reference Guide to Molt in North American Birds* (Houghton Mifflin Harcourt, 2010).

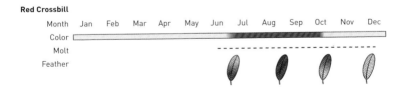

Red Crossbill

	Jan	Feb	Mar	Apr	May	Jun	Jul	Aug	Sep	Oct	Nov	Dec
Month												
Color												
Molt												
Feather												

plumage patterns of first-year large gulls are so variable. To simplify, in many immature large gulls the color hormones change from producing brown (immature) to gray (adult) pigments, as illustrated by the following tale.

Once upon a time there were two immature Herring Gulls. One was raised on the coast of Virginia, where its parents fed it poor-quality food from the local dump; it grew weak juvenile feathers and then flew off to the sunny Gulf of Mexico for the winter. Its back feathers soon became faded and worn, and by early winter it had replaced its brown juvenile back feathers with brownish, patterned feathers that looked not that different from the juvenile feathers. It molted before the pigment switch turned from brown to gray.

The second gull was raised on the Canadian tundra, where it was fed high-quality fresh seafood all summer; it grew strong juvenile feathers and spent its winter on the Great Lakes, with mostly cloudy days. Its strong juvenile feathers lasted all winter, and by spring it started to attain a few new back feathers, which came in grayish and relatively unpatterned. It molted after the pigment switch had turned. These scenarios may help you make sense of the seemingly bewildering variation present in a flock of winter gulls.

MOLT IS YOUR FRIEND

At one level, an awareness of molt may simply mean appreciating how it can change the appearance of a common species, such as a raven molting its longest tail feathers, which could produce a squared tail like that of a crow. At another level it can help resolve the identification of cryptic species of storm-petrels that breed at different seasons.

The presence or absence of wing molt can often be seen when other more conventional field marks are not discernable, and it might be your first clue to species identification. For example, along the mid-Atlantic coast in late summer, a small white egret with wing molt could be a Snowy Egret or a Cattle Egret, but it would not be an immature Little

patterned, browner
feathers, molted earlier

worn and faded juvenile
feathers, not molted

plainer and grayer
feathers, molted later

This first-winter California Gull shows rather variable patterning on its back, which reflects the interplay of molt timing and pigment deposition. A single and often protracted molt of head and body feathers occurs from the first fall through winter and into spring. Many new feathers are patterned and "immature-like," presumably attained earlier in the molt, whereas some of the longer scapulars are plainer and grayer, presumably attained later in the molt, after the switch to gray pigment had occurred. *Sonoma County, California, 12 March 2008.*

Blue Heron. By the time immature Little Blues molt their wings (at about a year of age) they have already attained a patchwork of slaty blue feathers; the white-plumaged juvenile Little Blues in summer and fall are not in wing molt.

How a bird's life is built around having a functioning coat of feathers is a fascinating subject, and there's a whole popular book written on molt, bringing it to life with lots of fun photos and examples.[2] Knowing something about molt can help you identify and appreciate birds, and it also leads us nicely into Step 11, the crux of most challenging bird ID problems.

This Bird Looks Different (Variation)

A s with humans, variation in birds can take many forms—variation in physical appearance, such as color and size, even shape; in vocalizations; in breeding behavior; in migration timing; in molt strategy; and in numerous other aspects of natural history. Step 11, variation, is perhaps the crux of all finer-level ID challenges, but here we limit the scope to variation in physical appearance.

Anyone who watches birds will notice, usually sooner than later, that not all birds within a given species look the same. Sometimes the differences are obvious and discrete, as between an adult male and adult female Northern Cardinal; sometimes they are more subtle, as between adult and juvenile Turkey Vultures; sometimes differences are average, as with female Red Knots averaging longer billed and duller red in breeding plumage than males, with only extremes readily assigned to one sex or the other; and sometimes plumage variation may seem almost infinite, as among first-year Herring Gulls.

OPPOSITE: Red-tailed Hawk is one of the most variable bird species in North America. In addition to obvious age-related variation, there is striking individual and geographic variation. This bird is a dark morph adult of the enigmatic population known as Harlan's Hawk, which has at times been considered a full species. Harlan's Hawks breed mainly in Alaska and winter mainly in the southern Great Plains. *Jefferson County, Oregon, 18 February 2011.*

Many misidentifications arise from not being familiar with the variations shown by common birds, which then get mistaken for rare birds. Developing an idea of how much normal variation occurs in a given species is something that comes with experience, the name we give to our mistakes. When might the variation you see indicate a different age, or sex, or even a different species?

In some cases, even considerable variation within a species may have little or no effect on your ability to identify it to species, as with California Condor, Brown Pelican, and Roseate Spoonbill. In other cases, even a slight variation might cause ID problems, as with juvenile sandpipers and immature hummingbirds.

Variation is a vast and complex subject, but it can be simplified by recognizing patterns. Here we consider variation in terms of five categories, which can work together: age, sex, seasonal, geographic, and individual variation.

AGE VARIATION

Obviously, nestlings and downy young look different from subsequent ages, but all North American bird species exhibit some degree of age-related variation in appearance even when they attain adult dimensions and grow their first coat of juvenile (or "real") feathers. The differences can be striking, and obvious at almost any distance (such as with Little Blue Heron and large gulls), or very subtle, best appreciated with a bird in the hand (such as the shape of outer primary feathers on storm-petrels).

Age differences can be apparent in one or more ways: for example, the color and pattern of plumage (most species), the length and structure of feathers (such as the central tail feathers of jaegers and the crest length of titmice), or the color of bare parts (such as eye color in some vireos and leg color in some gulls).

These age-related differences may hold for at most only a few weeks (as in many songbirds), or they may be apparent for a few years (as in

The drab juvenile plumage of Spotted Towhee looks very different from the striking plumage of an adult, but is not shown in most North American field guides. This plumage can be seen regularly in summer and fall, and could be quite puzzling. *Marin County, California, 27 July 2010.*

large gulls and some raptors). In general, larger birds take longer to attain adult plumage; most small birds resemble adults within a year, often within a few months.

Much of this age-related variation is covered in field guides, the major exception being the briefly held juvenile plumages of some songbirds, which can be seen in summer and early fall. Because these plumages are soon replaced by adultlike plumages, you don't see them for much of the year, but some of them can be quite confusing.

SEX VARIATION

Variation in appearance related to a bird's sex is quite frequent. In many species, the male is more brightly colored or strikingly patterned than the female. These differences may be shown year-round (as in quail, woodpeckers, and most warblers) or may be apparent only during the

The generally dark legs of American Pipit are a well-known ID characteristic mentioned in the field guides—yet juveniles, as shown here but not illustrated or even mentioned in most guides, can have very different, pale pink legs. Like many species, in late summer and fall the juveniles are also fresher and more neatly marked than the worn and faded adults. *Larimer County, Colorado, 29 July 2016.*

courtship and breeding seasons (as in most ducks, some sandpipers, and a few warblers). We know of no cases in which the sexes look different in the nonbreeding season but not in the courtship season. In a few species the female is more brightly colored, at least in breeding plumage, as with phalaropes. Belted Kingfisher is the only North American breeding bird in which females consistently appear more colorful year-round than males—but this is only a human perception, which may not relate to how the birds see each other.

In some species there is a marked size difference between the sexes, which may or may not be reinforced by differences in plumage. In most bird families, males tend to be larger, sometimes strikingly so (as in Wild

Turkey, Ruff, and grackles), whereas in others females are larger (as in most hawks, falcons, hummingbirds, and sandpipers).

For almost 60 percent of regularly occurring species in North America, however, males and females look basically the same throughout the year, at least to humans, and in many others the sexes look different only in breeding plumage. Although one sex often averages larger than the other, such differences are insufficient to reliably distinguish the sexes, at least in the field; examples include loons, petrels, cormorants, herons, rails, terns, most shorebirds, most flycatchers, crows and jays, wrens, most vireos, and most sparrows.

In most North American woodpeckers, the sexes look slightly different, usually with more red on the head of the male. The sexes in Williamson's Sapsucker, however, are strikingly different (female on left, male on right), so much so that ornithologists initially thought they represented different species. *Baja California, Mexico, 23 June 2015.*

SEASONAL VARIATION

Many species show a degree of seasonal variation in their appearance, which is sometimes linked to age and sex. Although the change from juvenile plumage to adult plumage is, in a sense, seasonal, it is a one-time deal, and the seasonal changes discussed here are the repeated, cyclic changes that occur each year in adult birds.

The commonest form of seasonal variation is a change in plumage color or pattern via molt, as with many ducks and shorebirds, a few warblers, and American Goldfinch. Striking seasonal variation can also come about through plumage wear, as with European Starling and Snow Bunting (see Step 10).

Because the impetus for molt is to replace worn plumage, not to gratuitously change plumage pattern or color (see Step 10), both sexes of a species undergo the same molts each year, even if one sex exhibits

Unlike most North American swallows, the sexes of adult Purple Martin (female on left, male on right) look quite different year-round. Purple Martin is also one of a handful of North American songbirds in which males do not attain adult plumage until their second year; in such cases, immature males resemble females or look intermediate between females and adult males. *Stutsman County, North Dakota, 11 June 2016.*

As well as their plumage pattern changing seasonally through wear, the bill color of European Starlings changes seasonally—from blackish in fall and winter to yellow in spring and summer. Birds also attain sex-specific coloration at the base of the bill—pale blue for males, pinkish for females. *Sonoma County, California, 26 February 2008.*

dramatic color changes and the other doesn't—for example, Scarlet Tanager. The main wing feathers are usually molted only once a year, which means that molt-related changes are typically apparent only in body feathers and wing coverts.

Seasonal variation can also occur in bare-part coloration, such as the facial colors of herons, or the bill color of European Starling, Fox Sparrow, and male House Sparrow.

LIFE HISTORY VARIATIONS COMBINED

As we've noted, variations reflecting age, sex, and season (which all relate to a bird's life history) are often linked. For example, males may look different in summer while females look the same year-round (as in Scarlet Tanager); immature males may resemble adult females in fall and winter, but by summer they resemble adult males (as in Townsend's Warbler); the sexes can look alike as immatures but different as adults (Painted Bunting); and the sexes may differ in breeding plumage but not in nonbreeding plumage (phalaropes).

The good news is that few species look different in every age/sex/ seasonal plumage combination. Moreover, often a pattern holds across a family. For example, loons and terns show distinct age and seasonal plumages, but the sexes look similar. Age/sex and seasonal plumages all look similar among storm-petrels (unless birds are examined closely, as with birds in hand), although immatures usually molt earlier than breeding adults (see Step 10). Among wrens there are no seasonal or sex differences in plumage, but juveniles look slightly different from adults, at least for a short period in late summer and fall before they attain adultlike plumage.

Almost as often there are one or two exceptions within a group. For example, in all North American finches the sexes appear similar year-round, once they attain adult plumage—except for American Goldfinch. In all North American flycatchers the sexes of adults appear basically similar—except for Vermilion Flycatcher. Being aware that in general there is no sex variation in flycatchers is knowledge that can help narrow your possibilities when puzzling over an unfamiliar flycatcher.

A good ID guide should summarize this information for each family, but simply by flipping through your field guide pages you can get a sense for the degree of life history variation shown by different groups. If your field guide doesn't provide this information, you could even annotate it yourself for each family—a useful learning exercise.

GEOGRAPHIC VARIATION

Many species of birds in North America vary in appearance across their geographic range. In some cases geographic variation may be minor, reflected by slight differences in size or plumage tones that are not readily apparent in the field. In other cases the differences may be quite

In Wilson's Phalarope, the sexes look different only in breeding plumage, with the female (at left) being brighter than the male. *Kidder County, North Dakota, 10 June 2016.*

noticeable, such that if an individual from region A turned up in region B it would be easily noticed among the typical individuals of that species in region B.

In many cases, variation correlates with climatic variables such as humidity and temperature. Biologists have at times proposed rules that link patterns of variation with environmental factors, such as Gloger's rule, which states that birds in wetter areas average darker than birds in drier areas. Thus, populations of various bird species in the dry Great Plains tend to be paler than average, whereas those in the wet Pacific Northwest tend to be darker than average. Examples include Merlin, Common Nighthawk, and Song Sparrow.

Geographic variation is usually more pronounced among resident species than among long-distance migrants, because the latter have a greater potential to disperse and mix their genes regularly. In some species, variation is clinal, meaning that although birds at one extreme of

Song Sparrow is one of the most geographically variable bird species in North America, both in size and plumage coloration. Unless you live in the desert Southwest, your local Song Sparrows probably don't look much like this individual (also see p. 114). *Imperial County, California, 27 April 2014.*

the range look quite different from those at another extreme, the change between them is gradual, and no lines can be drawn to mark where changes occur.

For a birder, the best reference for showing geographic variation in North American birds is *The Sibley Guide to Birds* (first edition).[1] Only geographic variation likely to be noticeable to birders is covered, and the standardized format (uncluttered by the extraneous rarities of the second edition) makes this variation fairly easy to assimilate.

The Minefield of Subspecies

Sooner or later, most birders come across the term *subspecies,* a concept that is often used to describe geographic variation. As with species (Step 1), it is important here to remember the word *concept.* We'll discuss subspecies here, if only to explain that birders would do well to avoid falling into the trap of trying to place formal subspecies names on many birds they see.[2] Really? Yes, really. Read on.

First, what is a subspecies? As with species, the definitions of subspecies have varied with different authors and at different times in history.[3] A subspecies is an *arbitrarily defined, identifiable population below the level of species,* which itself is often an arbitrary, but nonetheless useful, distinction drawn on the continuum of evolution (Step 1).

A subspecies is formally identified by adding a third part (or epithet) to its scientific name. For example, the richly colored West Coast population of Red-shouldered Hawk (*Buteo lineatus*) represents the subspecies *elegans,* as in *Buteo lineatus elegans.* A subspecies is synonymous with a race, despite the colloquial term *human race,* which is used when people presumably mean human *species,* of any race, creed, or color.

Some ID guides[6] describe male Vermilion Flycatchers from Arizona (top row, subspecies *flammeus*) as "head and breast . . . red to orange-red, often with pale mottling," whereas Texas birds (bottom row, subspecies *mexicanus*) are "deep red, without orange or pale mottling." The differences, however, as shown on these American Museum of Natural History specimens, are average and subtle at best, unlikely to be discernable on a single bird in the field.

Thus, the race *elegans* means exactly the same thing as the subspecies *elegans*.

In essence, subspecies developed as morphological units, ones that could be identified in a museum tray by virtue of measurements and plumage. Subspecies were often described based on adult males, which in many species are more colorful than females, but they can also be based on female plumages or even seasonal plumages. For example, the three widely recognized subspecies of Short-billed Dowitcher are best separated in breeding plumage—in nonbreeding plumage they are often not distinguishable. Thus, a subspecies may not be identifiable in all ages or sexes, or at all seasons.

The resident breeding Song Sparrows in coastal Marin County, California, look like the left-hand bird, but in winter some different-looking Song Sparrows show up there (right). Without (or even with) direct comparison to a series of specimens, it is not possible to reliably give the dark migrant a subspecies name, and—no surprise—there is disagreement over how many subspecies of Song Sparrow should be recognized. Based on its dark plumage and large size, however, we can be pretty confident it comes from the Pacific Northwest rather than from the interior West, interior Southwest (see p. 112), or East of North America. *Marin County, California, 25 April 2012 (left) and 23 November 2015 (right).*

In principle (and often in practice), the subspecies concept is extremely valuable, but frequently it has been misused and misunderstood.[4] For example, it has been estimated that more than 75 percent of all subspecies described for North American birds on the basis of measurements would not survive critical examination.[5] But nobody is lining up to do the checking, and so the literature is cluttered with numerous subspecies names that often have little or no utility in the real world.

In a recent study, Savannah Sparrow went from having twenty-one subspecies down to six subspecies;[7] the same author subsequently regrouped the six subspecies into four species that included a total of seven subspecies.[8] These arbitrary, even idiosyncratic treatments completely ignored plumage coloration (which was used in describing most if not all of the original twenty-one subspecies) and exemplify how subspecies can quickly ebb and flow.

Despite all this, some field guides illustrate a bird and label it as *subspecies X,* which may not be wrong, but it is quite possible that other subspecies are, to all intents and purposes, identical in the field to subspecies X (these other subspecies may not be shown or mentioned, though). Understandably, this may mislead you to name a bird you see in the field as subspecies X because it looks most like the picture in the field guide of subspecies X. That's what we do with species, but it doesn't necessarily work with subspecies. It's like having a field guide that doesn't show all the species, so without an image of Carolina Chickadee you'd likely ID the chickadees in Georgia (wrongly) as Black-capped Chickadees.

Some birders believe that subspecies names have sanctity, and they worship at the church of geographic variation. But, as we've seen, most subspecies remain scientifically unevaluated, which might lead us to wonder if some birders are worshipping false gods. It doesn't hurt to be aware of subspecies, but there's nothing wrong with staying away from them until you feel ready (if ever) to walk into the minefield they represent.

LAST BUT FAR FROM LEAST: INDIVIDUAL VARIATION

No two human beings are absolutely alike, and the same is presumably true of birds, although in many cases the differences may be discernable only to the birds themselves, not to human observers. The last type of variation, then, is individual variation, which, in its myriad forms, provides the raw material that forms the basis for evolution.

Individual differences may exist in plumage coloration and pattern, in plumage wear and fading (a reflection of feather quality combined with environmental factors), in bill color, in eye color, in the length of a crest or of tail streamers. Some individual birds are brighter or duller, more heavily streaked, and so on. Hybrids, albinos, and other aberrant pigment conditions are further examples of individual variation.

The degree of individual variation varies among species and between families, and may also vary with age or sex. For example, hybrids are relatively frequent among hummingbirds, but rare or unknown among swifts. A flock of crows exhibits almost no individual variation, to our eyes, but for some immature gulls or juvenile sandpipers it seems that no two individuals look the same.

OPPOSITE: When we think about plumage variation in birds, we tend to think about warblers, hawks, or immature gulls. How about variation in Pine Siskin? This small, streaky finch shows little geographic variation in North America and, unlike most finches, not much sex variation. (Although *The Sibley Guide to Birds*[9] shows males with much more yellow in the wing than females, this is only an average difference, and many siskins cannot be sexed reliably in the field.) On the other hand, the juvenile plumage (bottom two images) is not shown in most guides. Here are six Pine Siskins from Marin County, California, in mid-July to mid-August, showing appreciable individual variation in both adults and juveniles in color, extent of streaking, and amount of yellow in the wings.

If you look carefully, you'll probably find individual variation in most of the common birds you see. Field guides simply don't have room to cover all of this, but an appreciation of this individual variation is a key to developing your ID skills.

17 July

17 July

11 August

11 August

24 July

31 July

Morphs in some species, such as Short-tailed Hawk (two adults shown here), are straightforward and comprise simply light or dark morphs. In other species, such as Red-tailed Hawk, several owls, and immature jaegers, the variation is much more complex, although for the most part humans tend to simplify variation into a few convenient categories. *Nayarit, Mexico, 12 January 2016 (left) and 28 December 2010 (right).*

In some species, individuals can exhibit one or more distinct plumage types (or morphs), which may be called *dimorphism* ("two morphs") or *polymorphism* ("many morphs"). For example, some populations of Reddish Egret feature a white morph, quite different from the typical dark (or reddish) morph. Among some owls there are gray, brown, and reddish morphs, which can occur in differing ratios throughout the population. Color morphs can be maintained in all ages (as in the egret and owls), or they may be present only in some ages (as in Long-tailed Jaeger—immatures are polymorphic, but adults come only in a light morph).

Individual differences may seem infinite, but technically they are finite. The twenty-six letters in our Western alphabet allow for an almost

It has been said that no two immature jaegers look alike, and certainly the array of plumage patterns can seem bewildering. In such cases, structural clues are important for ID, as with the stocky body, short neck, and small bill of this first-summer Long-tailed Jaeger. *Marin County, California, 11 August 2010.*

infinite number of words, and the thousands of genes and their combinations allow for much greater potential variation, which we are far from understanding. It may be that juvenile Western Sandpipers or juvenile Herring Gulls have, say, 11,360 plumage morphs, but anything more than a handful and most humans can't process it. It's much easier for us to simplify all this into light and dark morphs, or red, brown, and gray morphs.

As with most aspects of birding, the more closely you look, the more you see. With practice, you may be able to recognize several individual House Finches that visit your feeder, or each individual immature hummingbird. For example, a friend of ours, Keith Hansen, took video of Anna's Hummingbirds visiting one feeder for five days in September 2010. His 287 clips revealed 119 different individuals (identified by distinct plumage and molt characters), although rarely were more than five

---

White or diluted plumage patches (due to pigment aberrations) occur in many species. The results of this phenomenon can sometimes be puzzling, but everything else about this bird points to it being a Dark-eyed Junco of the "Oregon Junco" population. It's just a weird individual with atypical white head patches. *Marin County, California, 6 January 2014.*

birds present at any one time, and 85 percent of individuals made only one visit.

Individual variation is perhaps the biggest hurdle to mastering most of the truly challenging ID issues in North America. How much white can an adult Thayer's Gull show on its outer primaries? How dark can the primaries of a pure Glaucous-winged Gull get? How much pale mottling can a pure South Polar Skua show on its back? How dull can the flanks be on an immature Rufous Hummingbird? How dull and grayish can the edges of the wing coverts be on a juvenile Least Sandpiper? How much white can a Western Meadowlark show in its spread tail? And so on.

Your own powers of observation, combined with experience (and taking notes—see Step 12), can help answer some of these questions, but it's good to recognize that many of these questions have yet to be answered satisfactorily, by anyone.

In conclusion, variation is variable. Most species vary with age, some by sex, and a few by season. Quite a lot of species exhibit appreciable geographic variation, and all species exhibit individual variation.

The last three steps we've looked at (structure, plumage, and variation) involve details, but remember, the devil is in the details. However, before you jump in deep and get bogged down in these details, recall Steps 1 through 8, the underlying path that brought you to this point.

Write It Down (Notes)

Watching and listening to birds—observing them—is both fun and challenging. It opens up the world around you and gives you reasons to go to places you might never have dreamed of visiting. But then, as you see and identify more and more birds, do you try to keep track of what you see—each day, each year, in each location?

Each time we go birding or use a field guide, we are benefiting from the notes that other people took. For example, when you visit an area and learn that mid-May or the last week of September is the best time to see species X, that information was gleaned by people like you writing things down so that patterns could be discerned (see Step 4).

If you travel farther afield, such as to other countries, keeping notes and a list of birds for each place is a kind of journal that can bring back memories of places, events, people, and of course birds. There are lots of reasons to write things down, not least because memory doesn't improve with age. So how might you go about keeping notes?

Perhaps the simplest way to keep notes is to write the location and

OPPOSITE: It's great to be outside enjoying the moment and watching birds. Sometimes, though, you may want to stop and make a few notes about a bird you're seeing, about its behavior, plumage, or vocalizations; maybe even sketch it or write down some questions about it to look up later or when you get home. *Larimer County, Colorado, 29 July 2016.*

date next to each species' name in your field guide, to remind you of where and when you first identified that species. The next stage might be keeping a list of notable birds you see in your yard, or of what you see each time you visit a local park or reservoir. Or you might make notes about songs, calls, molt, or any number of things that interest you and catch your attention.

TRADITIONAL VERSUS MODERN?

The traditional way of keeping notes is to write by hand in a notebook or journal. This can involve both a field notebook (something you always have with you in the field) and a field journal (something you transfer notes to at the end of the day, organizing them and making them neater).[1] The field notebook is also a place you can sketch birds and write descriptions of songs and calls while actually observing birds *in the field*.

The modern approach is to use a computer program to keep notes for you. You can even enter your lists in the field as you go, but in most cases that's all people do—keep lists of species. There's little attention to taking notes or making sketches, despite the fact that some programs can incorporate these things, along with your photos, videos, and sound recordings.

Many people find that a hybrid approach is a good compromise: write notes by hand in a field notebook, when it's easy to make sketches, record observations about weather, and scribble down questions; then enter a final and complete list into a computer program at the end of the day.

Photography is an increasingly popular way of birding. Although digital images can be helpful for documentation and reference, be aware that observation mostly stops when you put your eye to the viewfinder; don't forget to watch as well as click. Examining images later also allows you to see things you didn't notice in the field, and enables you to learn and to look for those features next time. As a rule, a combination of notes and images is the best way to go.

Steve started out keeping notes by hand, and he continues to do so. Here's a box of his field journals—in habitat, a field! These notebooks span the years 1999 to 2015 and have contributed the basic information for a number of identification articles and even books.

All too often people send us poor images of a bird and ask what it is. If those same people had actually observed the bird in the field, made some notes and sketches, described the voice, paid attention at the time, then the bird might be identifiable—but from lousy digital images alone the bird often cannot be identified and the record is consigned to the trash can.

An increasingly popular option for keeping notes is eBird,[2] a free online checklist program that allows you to record what you see in the field, upload photos and sounds, make notes, and keep all your bird lists up to date in the process. This versatile system allows you to keep lists for areas as small as your yard and as big as the world. It also adds your lists into a huge database along with everybody else's lists to provide openly available information on the status and distribution of birds worldwide.

The handwritten field notebook pages contain sketches and notes distinguishing Long-billed and Short-billed Dowitchers.

As well as helping you learn status and distribution, a field notebook can help you hone your powers of observation as you watch and sketch birds. Your sketches don't have to be works of art, they just need to be functional. Lots of people say, "I can't draw birds," but really, all it takes is time. These notes, made while observing both species together in nonbreeding plumage, helped Steve develop a sense of how to distinguish Short-billed Dowitcher from Long-billed Dowitcher, even when they're sleeping. *Wakulla County, Florida, 21 October 1981.*

Between eBird and writing notes longhand there lie many other options, too many to cover here. As with so many things in life, a good approach is to ask other birders what they do and get a sense for the pros and cons of each approach and each program. And, perhaps with a bit of trial and error, you'll find what works for you.

These are sketches of Steve's first-ever sighting of a Henslow's Sparrow, made in the field while watching the bird for over an hour. At the time, these notes helped reinforce what this species looked like; years later they help jog his memory about a great day in the field. *Point Pelee, Ontario, Canada, 5 May 1982.*

THE NEGATIVE SIDE OF LISTS

A complete list of what you see on a given day, or at a given site, is much more than that. It also reveals *what you don't see,* which can help you understand patterns of seasonal distribution at any scale, or perhaps learn about habitat preferences, or appreciate variation between years.

Many years ago, a crusty and idiosyncratic ornithologist, Allan R. Phillips, pointed out that birdwatchers "see everything," even some birds that aren't there. But, he realized, if they consistently fail to record a species, especially a fairly conspicuous one, then that's a pretty good indication it really isn't there. Thus, he used Christmas Bird Counts[3] to help

Checklist S30643115

◄ Older   All Checklists   Newer ►

| Location | Pt. Pinos--Seawatch, Monterey County, California, US [Map] [Hotspot] | Edit Location |

🖨 Print

📄 Download

✉ Email Yourself

❌ Delete

| Date and Effort | **Sun Jul 10, 2016 3:21 PM** | Edit Date and Effort |

Protocol:	Stationary
Party Size:	2
Duration:	1 hour(s), 59 minute(s)
Observers:	Brian Sullivan , Paul Fenwick List
Comments:	
	Submitted from eBird Android 1.2.3

👥 Share w/ Others in Your Party

➦ Send link via: 🆕 💬

Submit another for...

Same location and date
Pt. Pinos--Seawatch, Monterey County, California, US on Sun Jul 10, 2016

Same location
Pt. Pinos--Seawatch, Monterey County, California, US

Same area and date
Another location near Pt. Pinos--Seawatch, Monterey County, California, US on Jul 10, 2016

Same area
Another location near Pt. Pinos--Seawatch, Monterey County, California, US

Same date
Sun Jul 10, 2016

Different location and date

☐ Hide from eBird Output ?

⤳ Change Portal

| Species | **21 species (+2 other taxa) total** | Hide Media Edit Species List Review List |

| **1 Surf Scoter** | | Remove Species Review |

Age & Sex		Juvenile	Immature	Adult	Age Unknown
	Male			1	
	Female				
	Sex Unknown				

| **7 Black-footed Albatross** | Remove Species Review |

| **1 Murphy's Petrel** | Remove Species Review |

BLS notes: Viewed through Swarovski scope at 30X for approx. 45 secs; photos not attempted. First picked up moving SSW toward us out of the center of the Bay at a great distance, getting close enough to see details of the underwing, but not the face/bill. Immediately different, based on highly dynamic flight style compared with nearby Sooty Shearwaters. Slightly smaller, slimmer, and more angular than Sooty Shearwater, with crooked wings and sweptback 'hands'. Flight showed higher, steeper arcs, with wings tipping beyond vertical at the apex of each arc. Nearby Sooty Shearwaters were arcing lower and flattening out at the apex, usually flapping on the downward side. This bird did not flap during the entire observation. As it turned more SW to round the point, the underside became visible. All-dark below, including underwing coverts, with pale, jaeger-like flashes at the primary bases. Upperparts appeared all-dark brown at this distance. The bird was obviously molting inner primaries, and there were visible gaps in the wings here. I could not make out any pale around the base of the bill, though I tried to see that field mark. I made these notes and the attached sketch before consulting my reference material. Recent experience with this species (May 2016) helped solidify the identification under less than ideal viewing conditions. I considered other all-dark Pterodromas, but I believe size and structure in direct comparison rule out other rarer possibilities.

***Paul Fenwick notes: Our sea watch was set up in the traditional location just east of Point Pinos proper looking north. The bird was initially found by BLS mid-bay heading in a southward direction. BLS was able to get me on the bird which then changed course to a south-southwest direction. Total viewing time was approximately 45 seconds to one minute in duration. The bird was lost just north of the red buoy and we were both unable to re-find it.
The bird presented overall dark top and bottom. It was in obvious inner primary molt on both wings which revealed the pale bases on the outer primaries. The wrists of the bird appeared to be held forward and in line with the head. The outer wing was swept sharply backwards. No additional ID features could be seen on the bird.
The bird flew on the outer edge of the Sooty Shearwater flight line. This flight path allowed for direct comparison in size and flight style to the Sooty Shearwaters. My overall size impression of the bird was that it was slightly smaller than a Sooty Shearwater. The significant difference of the Murphy's Petrel was its flight pattern. The arc pattern was significantly tighter than that of a Sooty Shearwater and completed in a rhythmic pattern. The terminal peak of the arc was approximately one half higher that that of the Sooty Shearwaters. The ascent and descent pattern of the Murphys Petrel arc was similar. The Sooty Shearwaters arc was much more elongated with the bird rotating and flattening out at the top of the arc then gliding back to the water's surface.

ABOVE & OPPOSITE: We've mentioned eBird numerous times, but what does an eBird checklist look like? Well, here's a screenshot of part of one of Brian's checklists, from an interesting couple of hours sea-watching in Monterey County, California. You can note age and sex, scan your own field sketches, type in whatever other notes you like, and link the list to your photos and recordings, which are then archived in the Macaulay Library at Cornell. Your lists will also be updated automatically with taxonomic changes, such as species splits, and the whole database is free for anyone to use.

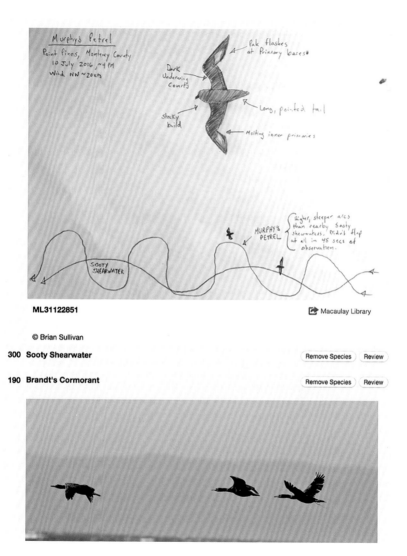

ML31122851

© Brian Sullivan

300 Sooty Shearwater   Remove Species   Review

190 Brandt's Cormorant   Remove Species   Review

establish the previously unknown migratory status of Green-breasted Mango in northeastern Mexico.

You can even make this a game, looking for "holes" in your lists and trying to figure out why. Why didn't I see any Eastern Phoebes this month? Why have I never seen California Towhee at this (seemingly suitable) site, when they are common just a couple of miles away? With eBird you can even pull up bar charts for any area with enough lists to help you discern these patterns.

WHAT SHOULD YOU WRITE?

However you decide to keep notes—and we encourage you to do so— there are some basic things to record on each birding trip. The simplest package would be location, date, and species of interest seen and heard. Ideally, though, you would also include start and end times, weather, and a complete list of species recorded with approximately how many of each. To this you could add notes on habitat, other birders you were with or met, and notes on the age, sex, vocalizations, behavior, molt, or whatever interests you for this or that species.

We can see you thinking: "Hey, hang on a minute, that sounds like a lot of work. And didn't I get into birding because it was an escape from work, an opportunity to enjoy the world of nature away from my desk, away from my computer?" And there's the rub: if you keep the kind of field notes that professional birders do, it really is work. On some trips, we have been up until after midnight, writing notes, going through recordings, editing and labeling photos—it's exhausting, especially when you're getting up again at 5 a.m. the following day!

Basically, it's all a matter of how we choose to use our time. Keeping notes in any form takes time, and contrary to what some advertisements would have you believe, you can't save time, you can only spend it. So spend it the way you would like. Many people enjoy watching birds with no strings (and no notes) attached; others make some notes or keep lists. If you do make notes, don't let somebody else make you feel your notes aren't good enough—they're whatever you want them to be. If you have time, write it all down. If you don't, pick and choose. Whatever you do or don't do, however, the main thing is to enjoy birding.

And on that note we conclude our twelve-step program. We hope the information contained here has been interesting and entertaining, answered a few questions, and perhaps even raised some questions. Now it's time to put the book down and go into the field!

Summary

Before you race out into the field, let's conclude by summarizing our twelve-step program and picturing how the steps might work together. You wake in the morning, grab a cup of coffee and a quick breakfast, throw some snacks and water in your bag, and head out to one of your favorite spots, a coastal lagoon in central California. Presumably, by this time you're awake enough to distinguish a bird from a mammal or a utility line fixture (**Step 1**), though don't be embarrassed or disappointed when that raptor shape on top of the hill turns out to be a rock you've mistaken before for a perched hawk.

You arrive at the parking lot knowing where you are (**Step 2**), plus the habitat (**Step 3**) and the date—October 2 (**Step 4**). It's a while since you've been to this location, so the previous evening you checked your field guide and eBird to prepare for what you might expect to see there at this season (**Steps 2 through 4**): "Oh, right, this is when the diving ducks start showing up; there should still be some migrating shorebirds around; and, wow, Red-throated Pipit is a rare possibility . . ."

You get to the lagoon's south shore. It's a clear, sunny day, with a light onshore breeze. There are some ducks fairly close out to the west, and a group farther out in the lagoon to the east. You stick with the closer group because they're both nearer and in better light (**Steps 5 and 6**). Among the

OPPOSITE: Here's a perfectly typical adult male Blue Grosbeak, yet you won't find a bird like this in your North American field guides. This male is in fresh plumage, seen briefly in fall in North America but commonly during the winter, south of the US. By spring, the brownish feather tips abrade to reveal the glossy royal blue shown in most guides. *Jalisco, Mexico, 9 January 2017.*

nearer ducks are a few dozen birds along the shoreline, dabbling at the surface, and another group a little ways offshore, diving (**Step 7**). Some of the ducks by the shore are making soft, slightly burry whistling calls, but you don't hear the diving ducks at all (**Step 8**).

At this point, your choices are narrowed greatly, and you're close enough to assess details. Starting with the dabbling ducks, you pick out one of the brighter birds and see it has a small bill, rather rounded head, short neck, and pointed tail (**Step 9**). It's pinkish brown overall with a pale grayish head that has a broad metallic green band through the eye and a big creamy forehead patch (**Step 10**). The behavior, whistling calls, shape, and plumage all fit male American Wigeon, a species to be expected in this location at this season. An experienced birder might make this ID in a split second, whereas a beginner might take some time over it, but either way it's a solid ID and something to feel good about.

How about the other ducks? Several of them don't have green or creamy patches on their heads, just an overall freckled grayish pattern, which can appear pale in direct light, duller and even vaguely brownish in indirect light (**Step 5**). However, their size and structure look like the male American Wigeon's (**Step 9**), and they're feeding in the same manner (**Step 7**). You check the field guide—females and males look different (**Step 11**), so these are female American Wigeon. You continue observing the flock, noticing small variations among different birds, and then: "Hey, this duck has a deep rusty head, unlike male or female American Wigeon, but it's similar in size, shape, and behavior. What is it?"

You pull out your notebook and camera to document the bird (**Step 12**). You run through Steps 2 through 11, and, checking the field guide, see that a second species of wigeon occurs rarely along the West Coast, and it has a rusty head—Eurasian Wigeon. Except your bird doesn't look quite like the picture in the book: it's brighter than a female Eurasian Wigeon and has a big white wing patch like a male, but it has a duller head than a male, without a buffy forehead patch. Given the variation you've seen in American Wigeon (**Step 11**), you suspect some form of

Observation and documentation comprise more than clicking a camera button. Having picked out a different-looking duck, you approach to get some photos, but the birds swim farther out and into worse light, and this is the best image you get. While this photo supports your ID as a Eurasian Wigeon, it's not conclusive. Writing some notes and describing the bird, its behavior, perhaps its voice, and maybe even making some crude sketches would help you (or others) to resolve the ID later. Ideally, write these notes while watching the bird, or immediately afterward, before your memory has time to fade. *Marin County, California, 2 October 2013.*

variation accounts for these discrepancies, but as you've never before seen Eurasian Wigeon you gather as much information as you can to help resolve the ID later. That done, you can continue birding, check out those diving ducks, and perhaps even find a Red-throated Pipit . . .

Later, you get home and consult some references, learning that your bird fits a male Eurasian Wigeon, but not one in full breeding plumage. You also learn that although both adult and immature male American Wigeons have white wing patches, an immature male Eurasian lacks the big white patches. So your bird, with its big white wing patch, was an adult male.

At close range, an adult male Eurasian Wigeon (right) in full "breeding plumage" (perhaps more accurately termed "courtship plumage") is stunning and straightforward to identify (male American Wigeon at left). But you don't always see textbook birds and plumages. *Marin County, California, 30 December 2015.*

But why were the male American Wigeons in full breeding plumage and not the Eurasian? Further research shows that many ducks in East Asia breed and molt up to a month or so later than in western North America, an interesting fact that adds unexpected support to your ID. By following the twelve steps, you have plenty of information to share, enriching your understanding and perhaps helping to teach others.

Acknowledgments

Over the course of our birding we have encountered and learned from many people who, in different ways, have influenced our understanding of birds, birding, and the natural world.

Steve. I am indebted to birding mentors and friends in my formative years of observing birds in Britain, including Al Venables, Laurel Tucker, John P. Martin, Will Wagstaff, Maurice Chown, and Peter G. Lansdown. Since leaving the UK, many people have helped me think about birds in different ways, including David Ainley, Jessie Barry, Ned Brinkley, Elaine Cook, Chris Corben, Renée Cormier, Dave DeSante, Jennie Duberstein, Jon L. Dunn, Ted Floyd, Geoff Geupel, Catherine Hamilton, Keith Hansen, Burr Heneman, Catherine Hickey, Rich Hoyer, Lisa Hug, Diana Humple, Ian Lewington, Michael O'Brien, Brian Patteson, Allan R. Phillips, Peter Pyle, Will Russell, David Sibley, Larry Spear, Kate Sutherland, Guy Tudor, Janet Visick, Sophie Webb, Wendy Willis, and Chris Wood; plus numerous interns at the Palomarin Field Station of Point Blue Conservation Science, California; participants on birding tours I have led worldwide for WINGS; and many young birders at events sponsored by ABA, Leica Sports Optics, and WINGS.

Brian. From an identification perspective, I was brought up through the "Cape May School of Birding," where figures such as Pete Dunne, David Sibley, and many others helped me learn how to identify birds using more than the marks laid out in traditional field guides. Their influence shaped the way I looked at birds then, and still do today. The team of people I work with now at the Cornell Lab of Ornithology made me realize that birding could be more than fun—that the information birders collect is valuable and can be used by scientists and conservationists around the world, as we do with eBird.

For review and comments on parts or all of the manuscript we thank Ned Brinkley, Renée Cormier, Mark Dettling (who suggested and ghost-wrote a framework for the summary), Jennie Duberstein, Paul Fenwick, Diana Humple, Michael O'Brien, Nathan Pieplow, and Peter Pyle. The Leica Birding Blog and the American Birding Association Blog have hosted some of this material in a slightly different form.

Notes

STEP 1

1. Steve N. G. Howell, "Never Mind the Bullock's—Taking Molecular Studies with a Grain of Salt," *ABA Blog,* April 10, 2013, http://tinyurl.com/d4ulh2o.
2. N. Collar, "A Species Is Whatever I Say It Is," *British Birds* 106(3) (2013): 130–142.
3. American Ornithological Society, http://checklist.aou.org.
4. F. B. Gill, "Species Taxonomy of Birds: Which Null Hypothesis?" *Auk* 131 (2014): 150–161.
5. IOC World Bird List, www.worldbirdnames.org.

STEP 2

1. American Birding Association, *North American Birds,* www.aba.org/nab/.
2. Cornell Lab of Ornithology, *eBird,* www.ebird.org.

STEP 4

1. Cornell Lab of Ornithology, *eBird,* www.ebird.org.

STEP 8

1. David Allen Sibley, *Sibley's Birding Basics* (New York: Knopf, 2002).
2. Nathan Pieplow, "Describing Bird Sounds in Words," *Birding* 39(4) (2007): 48–54, https://www.aba.org/birding/v39n4p48.pdf.

3. Cornell Lab of Ornithology E-Store, http://store.birds.cornell.edu/Raven_Lite_p/ravenlite.htm.

4. Cornell Lab of Ornithology Macaulay Library, macaulaylibrary.org.

5. Xeno-canto, www.xeno-canto.org.

6. Steve N. G. Howell, "California Condor: Seen Only?" *Birding* 47(3) (2015): 20.

7. W. R. Evans and M. O'Brien, *Flight Calls of Migratory Birds: Eastern North American Landbirds* (Old Bird, Inc., 2002) (CD-ROM); and A. Farnsworth, "Flight Calls and Their Value for Future Ornithological Studies and Conservation Research," *Auk* 122(3) (2005): 733–746A.

STEP 9

1. Roger Tory Peterson, *Peterson Field Guide to Birds of North America* (Boston: Houghton Mifflin, 2008).

2. David Allen Sibley, *The Sibley Guide to Birds* (New York: Knopf, 2000).

3. Kenn Kaufman, *Kaufman Field Guide to Birds of North America* (Boston: Houghton Mifflin, 2000).

4. National Geographic Society (NGS), *Field Guide to the Birds of North America,* 6th edition (Washington, DC: NGS, 2011).

5. Steve N. G. Howell and Sophie Webb, *A Guide to the Birds of Mexico and Northern Central America* (New York: Oxford University Press, 1995).

STEP 10

1. Steve N. G. Howell, *Peterson Reference Guide to Molt in North American Birds* (Boston: Houghton Mifflin Harcourt, 2010); and S. N. G. Howell, C. Corben, P. Pyle, and D. I. Rogers, "The First Basic Problem: A Review of Molt and Plumage Homologies," *Condor* 105(4) (2003): 635–653.

2. See first entry in note 1 above.

STEP 11

1. David Allen Sibley, *The Sibley Guide to Birds* (New York: Knopf, 2000).

2. Steve N. G. Howell, "On Avian Subspecies: Buyer Beware?" *ABA Blog,* April 16, 2012, http://tinyurl.com/7skxfb9.

3. See note 2 above.

4. See note 2 above and note 5 below; K. Winker, "Subspecies Represent Geographically Partitioned Variation, a Goldmine of Evolutionary Biology, and a Challenge for Conservation," in *Avian Subspecies,* (K. Winker and S. M. Haig (eds.), 6–23. Ornithological Monographs series, no. 67 (Oakland: University of California Press, 2010), 62–78 and 6–23.

5. Remsen, "Subspecies As a Meaningful Taxonomic Rank in Avian Classification," *Avian Subspecies* (K. Winker and S. M. Haig, eds.), 62–78. *Ornithological Monographs,* number 67, 2010.

6. P. Pyle, *Identification Guide to North American Birds, Part 1* (Bolinas, CA: Slate Creek Press, 1997).

7. J. D. Rising, "Geographic Variation in Size and Shape of Savannah Sparrows (*Passerculus sandwichensis*)," *Studies in Avian Biology* 23 (Camarillo, CA: Cooper Ornithological Society, 2001).

8. J. D. Rising, "Genus *Passerculus*," in *Handbook of the Birds of the World,* volume 16, J. del Hoyo, A. Elliott, and D. Christie (eds.) (Barcelona: Lynx Edicions, 2011), 550–551.

9. See note 1 above.

STEP 12

1. Steve N. G. Howell, "What Exactly Is a Field Notebook? (In 5 Parts)," *The Eyrie,* July 26, 2015, http://tinyurl.com/hldqmz6.

2. Cornell Lab of Ornithology, *eBird,* www.ebird.org.

3. Each year, around Christmas, volunteers help conduct a "bird census" and report their results to the Audubon Society. Read more about it here: www.audubon.org/conservation/science/christmas-bird-count.

Further Reading

There are many books written about birds and birding, plus numerous websites and blogs devoted to the subject. A lot of them are just plain awful, however, and should never have been published or created. To help you separate wheat from chaff, we suggest the following, somewhat eclectic selection as starting points for your further explorations into the world of birds and birding.

Better Birding: Tips, Tools, and Concepts for the Field, by George L. Armistead and Brian L. Sullivan (Princeton University Press, 2015). Aims to build your birding skills via a wide-angle approach. Covers traditional elements such as plumage, but also helps create context around each bird, including details of habitat, behavior, and taxonomy—all integral to identification, but often glossed over by field guides.

The Birder's Handbook: A Field Guide to the Natural History of North American Birds, by Paul Erlich, David S. Dobkin, and Darryl Wheye (Simon & Schuster, 1988). A handy reference to breeding biology, diet, and conservation status, with numerous interesting essays as well as species accounts for all North American breeding species.

A Dictionary of Scientific Bird Names, by James A. Jobling (Oxford University Press, 1991). A handy little reference that explains the derivation of the genus and species names for all birds in the world.

Earbirding.com. A website put together by bird sound aficionados Nathan Pieplow and Andrew Spencer about recording, identifying, and interpreting bird sounds.

eBird.org. As well as being an Internet-based checklist program built for birders by birders (see Step 12), eBird can provide maps and bar graphs of bird distribution for particular species, or for regions and by season —a useful tool for learning about what you might expect to find, and when, at any location.

Kingbird Highway, by Kenn Kaufman (Houghton Mifflin, 1997). One of the best books written about birders and birding, capturing the passion, dedication, and, most important, the element of discovery that drives us into the field each time we go birding.

Lives of North American Birds, by Kenn Kaufman (Houghton Mifflin, 1996). Identifying birds is great, but what about their life history? This book goes beyond the field guides to provide information on other aspects of birds' lives, such as habitat, nesting, feeding, and migration.

Macaulay Library of Natural Sounds, macaulaylibrary.org. A curated collection of sounds, photos, and videos of birds and other animals from around the world.

Merlin Bird ID. This free bird identification app from the Cornell Lab of Ornithology (merlin.allaboutbirds.org) walks you through five easy questions to help you identify your mystery bird. *Merlin* includes audio, images, and ID text for North America and can also identify a bird in a photo.

"On Avian Subspecies—Buyer Beware?" by Steve N. G. Howell, *ABA Blog,* April 16, 2012, http://tinyurl.com/7skxfb9. A summary of "the subspecies problem," written for birders in a nontechnical, even lighthearted vein.

Ornithology (3rd edition), by Frank Gill (Macmillan, 2007). There are numerous ornithology texts out there, some not worth the paper they are written on. This classic text offers a very readable overview of ornithology, accessible to anyone with an interest in birds.

Peterson Reference Guide to Molt in North American Birds, by Steve N. G. Howell (Houghton Mifflin, 2010). All you ever wanted to know about molt but were afraid to ask, with lots of fun photos and natural history reflections.

Sibley's Birding Basics, by David A. Sibley (Knopf, 2002). One of the best books written about how to find, observe, and identify birds; full of great tips and information.

The Sound Approach to Birding: A Guide to Understanding Bird Sound, by Mark Constantine and the Sound Approach (Sound Approach, 2006). A readable, entertaining guide to understanding the sounds that birds make. Lavishly illustrated, it also comes with two high-quality CDs. Written from a European perspective, but also very useful for birders in North America.

Xeno-canto.org. A collaborative website dedicated to archiving and sharing bird sounds from around the world. An incredible resource that can help you learn and appreciate bird vocalizations.

Photography Credits

Steve N. G. Howell: i, ii–iii, vi, 2, 4, 6, 10, 15, 18, 21, 23, 24, 26, 28, 31, 32, 35, 36, 37, 39, 42, 43, 45, 46, 47, 48, 50, 51, 52 (bottom), 54, 57, 58, 59, 60, 62, 64, 66, 68, 69, 70, 74, 75, 76, 78, 81, 82, 84, 85, 86, 87 (right), 88, 90, 93, 95, 96, 98, 101, 105, 106, 107, 108, 109, 111, 114, 117, 118, 119, 120, 122, 125, 126, 127, 132, 135, 136

Brian L. Sullivan: viii, 8, 13, 40, 52 (top), 72, 87 (left), 102, 112, 113, 128, 129, 146

Index

Page numbers in *italics* indicate illustrations.

morphs, 118, 120

Nighthawk, Common, 34, 97, 98, 111
  Lesser, 97, 98, *98*
North American Birds (journal), 20
North American Classification Committee (NACC), 16
notes, 122–31, 134. *See also* eBird
  field journal, 124, *125*
  field notebook, 124, *126, 127*
  negative side of lists, 127–30
  photography and, 124–125
  traditional vs. modern, 124–26
  what to write, 123–24, 130–31

oscine, defined, 68–70
Owl, Desert, 5
  Great Horned, *4,* 5
  Hume's Tawny, 5
  molt, 94
  plumage variation, 118

parrots, 8, 9
Pauraque, 76, *76*
Pelican, Brown, 104
Peterson, field guides, 10
Peterson, Roger Tory, 11
Petrel, Black-capped, 27
  size variation, 107, 110
Pewee, behavior, 56–58
  Boreal, 73
  Cooper's, 72, *72,* 73
  Eastern Wood, 56
  Western Wood, 56–57, *57*
Phalarope, plumage variation, 106, 110, 111, *111*
  Wilson's, 59, 61, 75, 111, *111*
Phillips, Allan R., 88, 127, 130
Phoebe, Black, 68
  Eastern, 130
  Say's, 47, *47*

photography, 124–125, 134
Pipit, American, 106, *106*
  Red-throated, 133, 135
Plover, Greater Sand, 23–25
  Snowy, 62, *62*
plumage, 90–101, 134
  aberrations, 116, *120*
  age variation, 104, 105
  color change through wear, 97–99
  color morphs, 118, 120
  color pattern and molt timing, 99–101
  juvenile, 105, *105, 106*
  seasonal variation, 108
  sex variation, 105–7
  terminology, 91–92
polymorphism, 118
Ptarmigan, White-tailed, 27
Puffin, Atlantic, *32,* 33
Pygmy-Owl, Northern, 14

quail, 55,
  variation, 105
Quetzal, Eared, 66, *66*

rails, sex variation, 105
rare birds, 22–25
raven, 63, 100
Raven Lite (software), 72
Redstart, American, 91
Roadrunner, Greater, 27
Robin, American, 60, 62–63
Ruff, 107

Sandpiper, Buff-breasted, 36, *36*
  Least, 121
  Marsh, 23, *23*
  Spotted, 35, 59, *59*
  Stilt, 59, 61, 75
  variation, 81, 103, 104, 106, 107, 116, 120, 121